SOMEWHERES IN
tHE MIDDLE

SOMEWHERES IN THE MIDDLE

A CREATIVE MEMOIR

by

Frank Gordon

Aesop Online Publishing, LLC
Livonia, New York

Published by Aesop Online Publishing, LLC. All rights reserved. No portion of this book may be reproduced in any form without permission from the publisher, except as permitted by U.S. copyright law. For permissions contact frankgordon91b20@gmail.com.

For further information check our website aop-frankgordon.com

The chapter titled "Angels All Around" originally appeared as a short story in *Narrative* magazine

ISBN: 978-1-7342514-0-1 Print version
ISBN: 978-1-7342514-1-8 Downloadable Audio
ISBN: 978-1-7342514-2-5 E-book

Editing: Michelle Scaglione and Ellen Henrie
Project Management: Della R. Mancuso
Art Direction: Donna Murphy
Front Cover: painting by author, "Out Wandering"
Back Cover: painting by author, "An Ideal Homestead"
    after the late Thomas Locker
Readers/Contributors: Michelle LaBarre and David Perkins, Janette LaBarre,
    Ben LaBarre, Jean Dutcher, Bev Galusha

TABLE OF CONTENTS

INTRODUCTION

There were twelve of us children living in a black house on a hill with parents who often disappeared, sometimes for days on end, leaving us to our own devices. Some current professionals might use the term "psychological maltreatment" to explain what we experienced, long term, on that hill. They might also describe our myriad family interactions as "dysfunctional." Throw in "co-dependent" and you'd have a perfect set. Truth is, I wouldn't quibble with any of those descriptors.

But for us kids, finding our way through the dense and suffocating fog of poverty, alcoholism, periodic abandonment, psychological and sometimes physical abuse, it was just a hardscrabble life—a fate that, by using all the creative ingenuity we could muster, we simply endured. After all, from attendance at school, we knew of several family situations far more difficult than ours. And one good thing we had going for us: in spite of the many dramatic arguments, a few group wrestling matches, and an occasional fistfight or unlucky kick to the groin, we had each other.

I was born in 1949 and grew up "somewheres in the middle" of this large, troubled family. With the "big kids" above me and the "little kids" below, surely we would find our way together. In this rather isolated world, the big kids helped the little kids and the little kids (usually) believed and did what the big kids told them. In this way, even when Ma and Daddy disappeared, the family unit stayed intact. Of course, in my youthful ignorance, there was no such thing as a "family unit"; there was just "the bunch of us."

Looking back, I'd say all of us, even "Ma and Daddy" with their many mysterious and irresponsible wanderings, had good (if not the best) intentions. It's just that some of us were, perhaps more than others, lost: lost in family dynamics that were too big and too complicated; lost in personal cravings and addictions that hurt and debilitated; and, yes, lost in introspective self-centeredness, an affliction of many who live and breathe in the mode of survival. After writing this book, I see more clearly that no one in this large and perplexing family of fourteen was so lost as myself. And I say that with no sense of blame or judgement toward others, nor even a hint of self-condemnation.

I wrote the book in the voice of myself as a young (preteen) boy. We're talking here about the "red-scare fifties" when many children truly believed nuclear bombs were poised to rock and shock us out of existence. The national news, coming at us from our black and white TV with its grainy screen and sporadic reception, talked regularly of the bomb; in school, like clockwork, the possibility of annihilation was made a vivid reality in monthly air-raid drills.

Well before the Cuban missile crisis, most school children were aware of the gruesome details of a nuclear blast and its horrible aftermath: sudden death, a mercy; the mushroom-clouded after effects of hot ash on tender skin, too horrible to contemplate. As we Gordon kids discussed the matter among ourselves, it somehow made sense that our little village just three miles away, our K-12 red-brick school building, and especially our black house, strategically located on the hill, halfway up that winding road, were likely targets.

My sister Bev became so convinced of pending incineration, she once refused to attend school for three weeks in order to stay home and protect our mother. She only relented and returned to school when my father threatened her with a visit to a psychiatrist. Today she says it was the word itself—psychiatrist—that scared her, and since she didn't know what it meant, she went back to school where, after a few days, her senses returned.

My brother Johnny and I attempted to dig more than one bomb shelter. Our plan was to make it deep enough so that when we threw ourselves facedown into it, the post-bomb ash would sweep right over. After hitting a few impossible rocks, though, we never made it much more than a foot below ground. A return to raucous play and fighting over toys usually provided an effective, if temporary, antidote to that and most other anxieties.

Besides the overarching fear of a nuclear holocaust and the ever-present worry that my parents might one day leave, never to return, early on I garnered into my anxious mind other pressing fears: nasty Russian spies crawling through the hills around our house—brandishing knives, no less; angry Indians on horseback, of the kind we saw in westerns on TV, mad at us because, years before I was born, Daddy had stolen their land. I knew I could do little to ward off Russian invaders and Indians, but how critical it became to address my biggest fear: the school nurse with her thick, dark red lipstick and shiny black hair, who had the power to break up our family and pawn us off to different homes. How crucial it was not to slip up in school and make her aware of our lack of food and care when Ma and Daddy went away.

And so, for me, early on, to avoid such exposure, there were many family secrets to be kept, important lies to be told, certain people (Ma and Daddy) to protect, and many outsiders to keep at bay or to avoid altogether. Among others, those outsiders would include, sadly, my successive grade-school teachers, the K-12 principal of our small rural school, and, of course, Johnny Gray, the village policeman who carried a gun when he wasn't wielding barber shears or delivering the mail.

By watching the big kids involved in creative cover-ups of our periodic abandonment, and by weaving my own faulty interpretation into events, I learned, in a myriad of conscious and unconscious ways, how crucial it was that we little kids never play it "stupid" in public and, above all, that we present the family in the best possible light. Early on I learned that fears and other more ambiguous emotions could be disguised or altogether suppressed. I also realized that most outsiders could easily be fooled, and that was a good thing because it seemed the only way to protect our hearth and home.

For example, when my parents were away and I missed the bus because, say, I overslept or couldn't find my shoes, the next day, for the sake of the family, I was willing to submit the required excuse from my mother (though in this case forged by an older sibling) stating that the real reason for my absence was diarrhea. Intuitively, I knew a note like that with a little too much of the wrong detail carried with it a necessary touch of authenticity.

So then, responsibilities for cover-up I could surely handle. But I worried about the younger kids who seemed clueless to the situation. And how often together we big and little kids stupidly blew our own cover: large group (and probably illegal) trips to the Salvation Army in the back of my father's old green stake-body truck; wild and disorganized attempts to catch the bus on time as, one by one, we lurched out of the house and bolted the quarter-mile journey to the bottom of our hill: how could anyone (especially the gawky-eyed "bus kids") watching our gross displays of social awkwardness miss the fact that we were poor and too often without adequate support and supervision?

About thirty years ago, when the first story (Hotdog Night) poured forth, my tears flowed just as easily as did the words onto the page: in fact, they wet the page considerably. From that point on, I knew to respect the young boy who was speaking through me and to allow him to tell his stories as he experienced, felt, and remembered them—the good and the bad—with no pressure from the adult part of me to correct the memories or to produce more.

I'm sure that in allowing young "Frankie" to speak through me the way I did helped me to uncover and sort out the many lies and confusions of my childhood, as well as heal some of the emotional wounds and pain I had incurred and buried along the way. Reliving my childhood in this way—reviving it, really— was in itself a form of healing, a corrective emotional experience, if you will; a long, gentle, though sometimes uneasy, journey toward centeredness and basic trust.

Because these stories were so personal, and because I had been so strongly conditioned to keep intact the family secrets, over the years as I wrote the various chapters, I shared them only with my close family, with no intent to publish, unless perhaps through my three grown children, posthumously. There were still, after all, at least in my mind, many secrets to be kept.

But with the slow acumen of aging, and by means of some effective therapy after my wife of thirty-seven years suddenly "disappeared" in a horrible automobile accident, I was better able to embrace the shame and pain of my formative years and to find some healing in sharing and discussing my early life story.

And so, it is with no little trepidation I offer Somewheres in the Middle to potential readers. My hope is that these stories offer some insight into the effects of poverty, abandonment, and abuse on kids, even though, with apologies to all, you will find herein no remedies. Perhaps though, one of these stories might trigger a thought, a feeling, a memory in you, the reader, and you will be encouraged to recreate your own life story, and, in that experience, find some healing, too.

Importantly, since these stories were written by the pro-verbial "child within" and since the boy didn't have a reader in mind when he wrote them, I think it might be fair to clarify who's who in the zoo of this large family of fourteen, as well as the several teachers in the order of my grade-school education. However, if you're the kind of reader who likes to piece things together, it is possible to read this book as if you are unraveling a mystery of sorts (after all, that's how I wrote it) and skip these next few paragraphs of information.

The parents were Elmer (born 1912) and Mary (born 1922). The children, eight girls and four boys, in order of birth, were Jean, Yvonne, Junior (Elmer Jr.), Charlotte, Bev, Johnny, Mary Lou, Frankie (that's me), Pearl, Grace, Lori, and Chuck. In school, the principal was the ever respected and feared Mr. Klump. The teachers (K-6), as each year they wonderfully appeared and paraded before my eyes, were: Mrs. Gaylord,

Mrs. Silvernail, Mrs. Lake, Mrs. Hollister, Mrs. McIntyre, Mrs. White, and Mrs. King. (Since the stories end about when I entered seventh grade, I won't mention the several teachers of junior high school who, in their devotion to helping all students, attempted, mostly in vain, to reach me, too.)

Finally, let me say that I have been hard-pressed to categorize the genre of this book, what I am terming a "creative memoir." Perhaps it would be better termed "mixed genre" in that it is as factual and true to life as I can make it, while allowing for the misperceptions, misinterpretations, and exaggerations of a wide-eyed child in a difficult situation. However, feel free to categorize the book as you please.

I've learned by comparing my memories with the sometimes-differing versions of my siblings that memory works in a most peculiar fashion: from decades past you call to mind a certain event, and what you can't quite piece together, the ever-helpful and imaginative brain fills in. I think this may be true for all of us. At any rate, after making a few comparisons with my family, where we differed, I always chose to stick with my own version of events, and of course, I encouraged my siblings to stay with theirs.

I am satisfied that even if these memories do not square with reality in every single detail of life in that black house on the hill, in the end it is true to the life I lived there, and, more importantly, it is true to the many beloved, and imperfect, characters.

Almost any childhood or social group you hold to the light will be full of good and mostly well-intentioned, though often troubled souls, who, after all is said and done, are more easily understood when not judged or condemned. I am sure it was my own personal need to accept my beleaguered past—a need to reconcile with it, really—that fueled this attempt to recreate my very early life.

For me, a degree of reconciliation with "days gone by" was probably more important than my ever-busy and sometimes mindless rush to the future; this reconnection or "reunion" with my past helps me live, in heart and mind, more peacefully. I know it heartens me to be able to look back at those sometimes overwhelming days of sad longing and fear, anxiety and personal loss, to see with new eyes the many brave and often comical souls who populated my little-boy world. Lately when I reminisce, unlike before I penned this curious account, it's often with a smile.

WHO It's FOR

Dear Missus Hollister,

We was at this church party and some lady comes up to me and says, "So you're Frankie Gordon!" Then she says you told her that I was the best boy you ever had in school. I look at her like she's crazy.

I say to her, "Missus Hollister meant somebody else."

She says, "No siree! Missus Hollister said Frankie Gordon was the best boy she ever had in forty years of teaching school!"

Now that doesn't seem right, so I say, "Well, she was just being nice."

Then she points her finger at me and says, "Young man! Missus Hollister means what she says and says what she means. And she never lies, even to be nice!"

So I say, "Well, what did I do that was so great?"

She says, "Maybe you don't have to do any great thing for Missus Hollister to think you're the best." Now that seems way off, so I figure I'll just run right outta there. And I was gonna run, but I feel sort of stuck, like she put a spell on me or like when we play freeze tag.

Then she puts her hands on my shoulders and says, "Oh dear, I didn't mean to upset you so." But her fingers is all nobby, so that breaks me loose, and I run away from her and all them crazy words.

But I couldn't stop thinking about what that lady said, Missus Hollister. When I was alone, I kept saying it over and over. It just didn't seem real! But I didn't tell no one what she said you said because they might laugh or say something stupid and take it all away.

So I kept thinking about what she said you said and wondering if you really did say it. Like when I was playing in the woods, I would cut off from the kids and go sit by Junior's tree and say it all again. I mean, how could I be the best boy you ever had in forty years of teaching school?

After a long time, I got really tired of thinking about it. But I couldn't make myself stop. I was like that crank-up clock on top of the piano. It just keeps ticking no matter what. So after lots of days of thinking on and on like that, with me trying to stop and not stopping, I got so I wished I'd never even seen that old church lady. I'd throw stones at these big trees and holler, "Why did you tell me what Missus Hollister said?" Or I would go, "Why didn't you keep your big mouth shut!" I never hated no one before, but it seemed like I did hate that old church lady. But really I was mad at myself. Kids aren't posta think like that all day. They're posta play!

So one day I was walking down the road, thinking about the same old thing I didn't want to think about, like how could I be your best boy in forty years of school? And did you really say it? But this time I got really mad. I said to myself, "Look here, you idiot! Nothing is gonna change, no matter how much you think about it. So why don't you just go ahead and believe Missus Hollister really did say it? Then it won't drive you so crazy!"

So right then and there I stomped my foot and hollered

right out loud, "Now you stop right now Fuzzy Head, because she really did say it!"

And that made me feel better right away because now I was just thinking one way and not two ways about the same thing. And right away I stopped hating that old church lady, too. Instead I would say things like, "She really did seem nice after all." Or, "Why would she make all that stuff up when she don't even know me?"

One day, after all that, I was walking down the road, throwing stones and whistling, and I laughed and hollered right out, "Missus Hollister really did say I was the best boy she ever had!" Then I knew I really did believe it, and I ran and skipped and jumped all the way home.

Then I got it in my head that I wanted to talk to you, like really bad, Missus Hollister. But you got old and don't teach school no more. And there wasn't no one to take me to your house because no one drives except Daddy. And I don't even know where you live anyways. Besides, I still didn't tell no one what you said, not even the big kids, or Ma.

So then I started to think about what I could do to make what you said about me come true in real life. I mean, how could I really be the best boy, just like you said? It seemed to me like I should do something really good because it wasn't right to have someone say you're the best and then not do anything to show it's true. I was playing by them small trees we bent over, thinking about that, when it popped into my head what you said to me one day in school.

You had me over by your desk. Everyone else was on the playground, but you kept me back. You was all excited about this story you made us all write for homework. It was about what we do in our family after school, and I wrote my story about hotdog night. You was pointing at it and saying I should write more stories like that to make a book because nobody has twelve kids in a family. You said you knew I could write a book, too, if you taught me how. But right then I just wanted to go out and play.

But you kept talking and talking and pretty much told me how to do it. I thought you were a little crazy right then, but now I'm not so sure. Now I figure maybe if I do write that book, it will make me the best boy ever, just like you said.

You said for me to write about the little things that the people in my family do—things we don't even think about, like how we get along, or how we call each other names, or how we walk barefoot, or how we wear each other's clothes. Or how Ma does all her work with twelve kids around. Like how she cooks or how she gets us ready for school, and who cuts our hair and how we catch the bus and things like that.

You said to be brave and write it all down and don't care what people might think. You told me even to write about when we do bad things. Like when Junior got in that big fight with Yvonne and Jean. Or when Johnny burned up our field. Or what happens when Ma and Daddy don't come home. Well, I was with Johnny when he burned up that field. And you said you would like whatever I wrote, no matter what.

You said to write how I talked when I was little, if that's what the story is about—even if it's bad writing. Like when people say 'ain't' at home—you said it's okay to write 'ain't' just like they said it. Or when Daddy says bad things, to write it like he says them. But you said I could only write them bad words in the book and not say them in school or on homework.

I told you then that I won't ever write 'ain't' or ever say it neither. But really, I just wanted you to let me go out and play. So when I said that, you did let me go. And was I glad to get away from you. But when I looked back, I saw you was feeling sad. I think that was because you knew I wasn't ever gonna write no book.

Right before I went out the door, though, you jumped up and grabbed this book off the shelf and ran over to me and showed me how to write one. Like, first you get a cover, and then you make a name for the book. Then say who you wrote it for. Then you have a page that tells you the name of each story, and what page each story starts on. And then you just write the stories and stick them on the page you said you would.

So, sitting there by those trees, remembering all that, I say to myself, "Oh, heck, I can do that!" And I thought how that would make you happy and maybe pay you back for saying such good things about me. And if I really did write that book, maybe I really would be the best, because there ain't no kid so little like me that ever wrote a book. There you go Missus Hollister! I wrote 'ain't.' Ain't you happy now? Ha-ha!

But I have to write upstairs when no one is looking. And I have to hide it because the little kids get into your things, and the big kids all make fun. There's this here place behind the wall where I put all my secret stuff. Daddy didn't build a real wall here yet, so I can crawl in behind these boards to write, just like I'm doing now.

There ain't no light bulbs way back in here, but the sun comes through these cracks in the house, so I can see good enough. But I can't write in winter because snow comes through the cracks and the wind blows right on through the house. So

I'll have to get it done before it snows.

So anyway Missus Hollister, here goes me writing my stories for you. I'll make them all true, just like you said. Maybe I'll start when I fell from that big high chair because that's what I remember first. Or maybe I'll write about how ascared I was when we first moved to New York up here on this mountain, and how the house looked so creepy at night, and how the owls made you think they was ghosts like Mary said was in the cellar. Or maybe I'll just start with "Hotdog Night" because you already gave me an A for that.

Anyway, I hope this is okay with you, Missus Hollister. But I know you will like it because you said you would like whatever I wrote, no matter what. And I know you will like it because you was always so nice to me, and you gave me all them good grades. Johnny said you gave them to me because I made you feel sorry. But I never told you we was poor. And I never told you or no teacher what Ma and Daddy do because you'll tell the sheriff and he'll take us all away. So why would you feel sorry for me?

So anyway, here's all my stories, Missus Hollister, from your best boy in forty years of teaching school. Ha-ha!

Frankie Gordon

P.S. Junior calls me "Fuzzy Head" for short—ha-ha-ha!

CHAPTER 1

HotDoG NIGHt

It was hotdog night when we always have hotdogs and you get your own bottle a coke. You suck on it until your tongue goes in the bottle and then it hangs there and you run around and everybody laughs! And tomorrow's no school for the big kids. And the Lawn Ranger's on TV. If it ain't broke.

Ma and Daddy bring lots of food on hotdog night, and when I see them driving up the road, I hold onto my peterbug and dance around and make funny faces and scream really loud. The little kids hold their pee things too and dance around when they see me do it. And it's really fun! I don't have to help bring in food because Jean says I'm too little. But the big kids all help.

When Ma comes in she says, "Now don't just dig into things," but we do anyway. The big kids put the bags down everywhere. And there's patata chips and coke and lots of bread and hotdogs and other stuff. Like there's flour and butter and pasketti and jars of jelly and peanut butter and spam and baloney.

Then Daddy comes in, but he ain't mad. He's just stomping snow off his boots. Then he really does get mad and stomps down cellar. And he hollers up at Junior, "You keep this fire going or I'll break your fecking neck!" Mary says I ain't posta say that, but who cares what she says anyways. Ma says she's only one year older, but she thinks she's big.

Everybody stops and shuts up when Daddy hollers. But pretty soon we all start talking and laughing and making noise again, and Junior comes back out from where he hid when Daddy hollered at him. It wasn't his fault the fire went out. We was all watching the Lawn Ranger and Tonto, and then Jingles and Wild Bill was on after that. Jingles hollers, "Hey Wild Bill wait for me!" He almost falls off his horsey because he's hanging on to his hat and shooting and riding all at the same time and everybody laughs. So Junior would've missed all that if he was down cellar watching the fire. And it's the kitchen stove that keeps you warm anyways, not the cellar one.

I miss mosta the stuff that's on TV because I want to see Ma and Daddy come up the road. So I go out to the big pitcher window and look for the car lights turning off the highway. When I see some lights, I run in and holler to the big kids, "Hey! Here comes a car up the road!" They all come running out to see if it's Ma and Daddy, but mosta the time it ain't. So they say, "Frankie, don't tell us there's a car coming unless you know it's really them."

Jean says, "Frankie you get in here and watch the Lawn Ranger and cover up!" But he don't shoot the bad guys mosta the time or holler Hi-O-Silver. And you can tell when he's gonna shoot because the music gets really loud and scary. Then you can run in and see him do it. I'm not afraid of those bad guys. And Tonto's good, too. So I stay out there by myself and watch the cars go by on the highway until they start to shoot. Then I run back in.

You can see lots of cars moving out the pitcher window, and you never know what one is gonna turn off the highway and come up our road. So when one does, I think it's Ma and Daddy, even if it ain't. But the big kids can tell if it's really them, even for the far-away cars. Like they say, "Oh, no, that's a truck," or "That one's got them new turning lights that blink," or "That one's going way too fast for Daddy!" Bev and Junior can tell best if it's really them.

Sometimes the car lights get all the way to the bottom of our hill, but they go right on by because it's not really them. When they get close to our road, I start saying, "It's Ma and Daddy, it's Ma and Daddy, it's Ma and Daddy!" until they don't turn up our road, and then I say, "It's somebody else's ma and daddy." Once I got a toothache and I kept saying, "It's Ma and Daddy, it's Ma and Daddy," and the toothache went away! So Daddy didn't have to pull it. We all know he really ain't gonna break Junior's neck. But Junior thinks he might, so he runs and hides until Daddy forgets that he was mad.

There's ice on the pitcher window when it's cold, and sometimes it gets really thick so you can't see out. There's a place on the window where there ain't no ice, but it's way high up, and I ain't posta stand on chairs. So I put my hand against the window where I can reach, and it melts the ice so I can see out just a little. Then I pull a chair over and get on it, but I don't stand up. And I put my cheek right against that spot where my hand was until the rest of the ice melts, and then I can see out really good.

I like to look out like that when the snow is falling really big and the cars go by. It makes you tired. Not tired like when it's time to go to bed tired. It's like you can't see nothing through that spot but the snow falling down. And it falls down really slow, like it's tired too. And the snow makes everything look really good out there. Like, why does the Lawn Ranger shoot people just because they rob a bank? They could give the money back! But the bad guys ain't so fast as the Lawn Ranger. So he's good.

It's really slow out the pitcher window. Chipper walks by wagging his tail, and he licks the snow, and then he just stands there like he's looking for Ma and Daddy, too. You can tell where he was walking because his tracks is so deep.

I say to Pearl, "Them tracks is slow!"

She says, "Tracks ain't slow. It's the snow that's slow, or the dog is."

I say, "No, the tracks is slow!" Like you can't see them fill up when you're looking at them. But even when you're looking at them, they're filling up. Like when Ma and Daddy go to the store. They leave them tracks walking to the car. And then the car leaves these tracks when they drive down the road. Well, I was watching them tire tracks.

So I say to Pearl, "I bet they come home before them tracks fill up."

She says, "Well, they might not come home."

I say, "You shut up, you!"

She says, "You can't make me!"

So I say, "That'll make Gracey feel bad, and she's only little."

And she says, "Oh, yeah!" But Pearl's only little, too.

After a while the tracks get really deep and go away. But they don't really go away because I can tell right where they was. That's because everything is slow out the pitcher window, and the tracks is slow. I like it when the snow is really big and falling down, and Chipper stands there looking down the road like he's watching, too.

Yvonne comes out and says, "God makes every one of them snowflakes." Charlotte says the angels help him. And Bev dances around and spreads out her hands like she's an angel making snow.

I go, "Sometimes the angels get mad and don't help God," but that makes them all laugh.

Charlotte says, "Nobody tells God what they're not gonna do, Frankie."

Bev says, "Well, the Devil does!"

Charlotte says, "I mean if you're a good angel you don't tell God what you're gonna do."

I say, "When they're mad you can hear them growl like Daddy's car on top of them trees!"

Charlotte says, "Frankie, angels don't get mad!"

But you can hear them growl on the mountain when they get mad. So I say, "They sound like Daddy's car when it's broke."

When the snow keeps falling down nobody can tell where the tracks was except me. Because I keep my eyes right there. It's like I can see right where Ma got in the car and looked back. I waved to her, and right then is when I said to Pearl, "I bet they'll be home before them tracks fill up."

Mosta the time they do come home. That's when I yell out and everybody comes to the pitcher window, and I get the little kids to laugh and dance. Daddy gets paid on hotdog night. And anyways, Junior keeps the fire going in the kitchen because wood burns easy. But he don't go down cellar so much because coal burns hard. So that's what makes Daddy say he's gonna break his fecking neck.

CHAPTER 2

HOW YOU MAKE HOTDOGS

There's a stove in the kitchen that's got these round iron things on top. You can lift them up with a handle to see the fire. Or you can pull the front door down to look in the oven. But be careful! It gets really, really hot in there. In case you don't know, the wood goes in the top part of the stove. But first you take the top part off, so you can put the wood in. But you have to be big to do all that.

You can put your feet on the side of the stove. That makes you warm when Ma's making hotdogs. You have to sit on the pile of wood to do that. Or you can crawl in back of the stove where Chipper sleeps. But be careful you don't touch that stovepipe! Daddy cut a hole right through the house when he put it in, and I watched him do it.

We have this big pan with a long handle that Ma puts water in. Then she puts it on the stove. After a while it gets real hot and bubbly. If you pull on the handle, the water falls on you. Then your skin falls off. Like when the Russians drop that bomb and the hot ashes eat you up. So we keep the little kids away from the stove.

Ma says to the girls, "You didn't put the water on like I told you."

And they say back, "Well, we didn't know when you was coming home!"

And Ma says, "It never hurts to put the water on, because you can always use it." Like for washing dishes.

But there ain't no dishes on hotdog night! That's because all you have is a hotdog to carry and some patata chips. You hold the hotdog in your hand and then you put the patata chips in your shirt like. So you don't need plates. But you can't carry the bag because it's big and everybody wants to get at the patata chips.

So I tuck some in my shirt. Then I go in back of the stove and sit on a pile a wood, with my hotdog. And—oh yeah—sometimes you have to carry a coke, too. That makes it really hard. Unless you ain't got any left, like me. I drink mine right down. But Pearl and Mary pig-save. That's so they can show off when mine's all gone. Just to be brats.

When the hotdogs get all done, Ma says "Frankie, you want butter or ketchup?" But both is good, so I have both. Then she says, "Now you go and sit down at the little table." But I go back in where Chipper sleeps. It's way too noisy out there, anyways. And the little table is for babies. Like the little kids always cry even when there ain't nothing to cry about. But I never cry. I mean I never cry like the little kids do, just for nothing. Well, one time Pearl bit me and I bit her right back. Then Ma hollered at me. So I cried that time. But I never cry on hotdog night. I mean, when they come home, I never cry.

When you sit back in there by Chipper, it's really warm and you can look out and see it all. Gracey pulls on Ma's dress. She's crying because she wants to get picked up. But you can't pick up little kids and make hotdogs too.

So Ma says to Charlotte, "Here, you take Gracey and hold her and cut her hotdog up." So Charlotte's got to wait for a hotdog. But she always does what Ma says. She just don't like

Jean to boss her. Like when Ma ain't home, Jean's the boss because she's the oldest. But Daddy's the real boss, even when he ain't home, and everybody knows that.

He sits out there at the table smoking, and he says something to Ma like what he's gonna do the next day. He don't like it when there's too much noise. You can tell he might blow up. So mosta them go in by the TV to eat. But he don't like it when everybody sits in there. That's because when he was little, he had to eat at the table. And there wasn't no TV. And you had to work a lot more than we do now. And he never could come downstairs in his underpants because they made him go right out to the barn before the sun came up. So they was mean to him.

I like hotdogs because you don't need help and you don't have to sit at the little table and you can run around. Well, you ain't posta run around, but you can because hotdog night is different than the rest. Daddy gets paid and comes home from work, and they get right in the car and go to the store. And we eat later, when they get back, so by then everybody's really hungry.

But when they don't come home, Jean says, "Well, maybe they got stuck in the snow or the car broke down." And she says not to cry because she can make hotdogs if there's any, or we can go and borrow some. But they weren't really stuck in the snow because sometimes they don't come home when it's summer. But I don't say that to Jean. She's only trying to make the little kids feel better, and that's good.

When Ma comes home, I give her a hug and say, "You make hotdogs the best!" Sometimes I eat two, but I give Chipper some. He likes to drink the hotdog water, too. Ma says I can give that to him after we eat and the water cools way down. But she says not to let him drink outta the pan. Ma says it takes two loaves of bread to feed everybody and enough hotdogs to fill that big pan right up! So anyways, that's how you make hotdogs on hotdog night.

CHAPTER 3

MISS SMARTY PANTS

Well, I was behind the stove with Chipper, and Mary comes back in there.

She says, "See my new shoes!" But they're not really new. Missus Gashay, who lives up the road, gave them to her. They're saddle shoes. They got this thing that looks like a saddle over the top of them where the shoestrings go. The saddle thing is brown, but the shoe part is white.

I say, "Daddy don't want you to have them."

She says, "He don't really care."

I say, "He's mad at Missus Gashay for giving them to you because she's poorer than we are."

She says, "Well, maybe God told her to give them to me."

So we were sitting there getting warm and I say, "I'll break your fecking neck!"

She says, "You didn't say that right."

I say, "I did too."

She says, "Well you ain't posta say it, anyways."

I say, "Daddy did!"

She says, "Ma will get mad if you say it."

So I say, "I'll break your fecking neck!"

She says, "You don't say that mister! And anyways, you still didn't say it right."

I say, "I did, too—I'll break your fecking neck!"

She says, "That ain't right!"

I say, "It is too right!"

She says, "No it ain't!"

I say, "Oh, yeah, how do you say it?"

She says, "I can't say it because Ma will get mad."

So I go, "You don't even know!"

And she says, "I ain't stupid!"

I say, "Well, you just said ain't."

So she says, "That ain't swearing."

I say, "Well, neither is, 'break your fecking neck.'"

She says, "It is too swearing, because people only say it when they're mad."

I say, "Being mad don't make it swearing. It's got to be like them other bad words to be swearing." Like that time I said 'titties' and Yvonne rubbed soap in my mouth.

But she says, "It is too swearing!"

So I say to her, "Well, I wasn't mad when I said it, so I wasn't swearing."

But she says, "You was pretending to be mad and that's just the same." But I wasn't pretending to be mad—I was just saying it like Daddy says it.

She says, "No sir! You were pretending to be like Daddy when he swore at Junior—and he was really mad!"

So I say, "Well, if you're so smart, what does it mean, anyways?"

She says, "Well, it ain't very nice. That's what it means."

So I say, "You won't tell Ma I said it, will you Mary?" Because I don't want Ma to feel bad.

She says she won't tell if I promise not to say it again, so I say okay.

And she says, "Cross your heart and hope to die." So I cross my heart and hope to die. But then she runs right out and tells Ma anyways, but Ma don't hear her because she's talking to Daddy and everybody out there's making so much noise from hotdog night.

So I holler out at her, "When you cross your heart and hope to die, you're posta do what you say!"

She hollers back, "I didn't cross my heart and hope to die—you did!"

Old Miss Smarty Pants. She always thinks she's right. Like, God didn't tell Missus Gashay to give her them shoes. He would've told her to give me a pair first, because she's just a brat!

CHAPTER 4

GETTING BREAD

Sometimes they don't come home on hotdog night, but they do later. Like the next day, or the next day after that, or the next day after that. Then you have to mind Jean and Yvonne and Junior. But sometimes Junior picks on us, and Jean has to make him stop because she's the boss because she's the oldest. Like one time, Junior got mad at me because I wouldn't go get bread. That's all the way to Missus Benets!

So I say, "I ain't going."

He says, "I go in the winter, so you go in the summer."

I say, "Ma says I can't go down the road by myself."

He says, "You just walk in the ditch and follow the road."

I tell him I ain't going, so he says, "I'll take you down the road. Then you go up to her house."

I say, "No! I want to chop wood."

He says, "You're too little."

I say, "I can too chop wood!" Like the flat kind you just break with an axe.

He says, "That's only kindling wood." So then he starts picking on me and trying to make me go down the road to Missus Benet's. And pretty soon he's picking on the little kids, too—just like he always does when he gets mad at Ma and Daddy. Some of the kids start crying, but I don't.

So Jean hears them kids crying and comes right out. She's got this big red hanky on her head for cleaning the house, and she's wearing them new glasses that look like cat eyes. And she's got this broom in her hand that she runs us down the road with before she cleans the house.

She tells Junior to leave us alone and hollers at him, "If you want bread so bad mister, go get it yourself!" Then she tells him they'll be home pretty soon, anyways. He says he ain't waiting until Christmas. And he says some bad words like Daddy does when he gets mad. Then he climbs up on the tractor. But now Jean gets mad and throws the broom down. She yanks him off the tractor and they start fighting.

So Jean calls out for Yvonne because she can't fight him all by herself. So Yvonne comes running out. They try to hold him down, but he's real fast. So Yvonne hollers out, "Someone go call the police!"

But we ain't got no phone, so they work together and trip him, and he falls down and they sit on him in the dirt. Then they call for Bev and Charlotte to help. So they come and sit on his legs so he can't kick at them no more.

When they got him still, Yvonne yells at Johnny, "You go up to Missus Gashay's and call the police!"

But Johnny says, "No! You get off Junior." So there's only little kids left to go, but we ain't posta go down the road. Well, they must of hurt Junior because he starts crying, and he's way too big for that.

So I say, "I'll go get bread." But no one hears me because they're making so much noise.

So I say to Mary, "Let's go get bread!" So we run down the driveway, but the little kids have to stay back.

I've never gone for bread before, but I say to Mary, "You just stay in the ditch and follow the road." So we do that. I holler for Mary not to run so fast because she's got shoes on and the stones is big. We have to hurry because you can hear Junior crying all the way down the road by where the Devil lives.

But when we get to the bottom of the hill, the road goes two ways, so we get down there, and Mary says, "Well, where's the bread?"

I go, "Missus Benet gives it to you. But you have to say we ran out and Ma will pay her back when she buys food next time."

Mary says, "I mean which way do we go for the bread, stupid?"

So I say, "Junior says you just stay in the ditch, so you go this way here."

She says, "Well what if he meant that ditch over there?" I say, "Well, Junior says you don't ever have to cross the road, so it's this ditch right here."

She says, "We got to hurry because they're hurting him."

I say, "But Junior's stronger."

Well, right then is when Ma and Daddy come driving up the road. Daddy stops the car by us and says, "What are you doing down here all by yourselves?" Only he swore.

I say, "Jean and Yvonne are holding Junior down!"

He says, "What the . . ." and he swore again about that place you go and burn when you die if you're bad. But Bev says you have to be bad all the time to go down there, not just once or twice, and little kids never go there.

So Daddy hollers, "You get in!" But there's no place for us to sit because the car's full of stuff from the store. So me and Mary stand in the back and hang on to the front seat—and that makes us laugh because Daddy starts driving really fast, and he's trying to miss the bumps and holes in the road, and we're back there sliding all around.

But he hollers back, "Now you kids shut up!" So now he's really mad.

When Daddy pulls in the driveway, he jumps right outta the car. Mom sits there and hollers, "Now Elmer, don't get carried away!" But Daddy has it all fixed by the time me and Mary get outta the car and run up to the house. Pearl told me he just hollered once, and everybody jumped right up, and right then Junior stopped crying. But that's when the girls all started in, saying how bad Junior was. So Daddy shakes up Junior, but he don't hit him. Then Daddy starts to laugh and says we're all a bunch of wild Indians.

When I get up there, Jean's crying, and she hollers at Daddy, "You should've come home last night so this wouldn't happen!"

Daddy says to Yvonne, "Don't you ever tell the kids to call the police."

Then Ma comes up and whispers to the girls, "I tried to make your father come home but he wouldn't."

So I pull on Ma's dress and say, "Well, where was you then?"

She says, "You know I don't drive." But I know she don't drive, I just wanted to know where she was.

The big kids bring the groceries in the house and pretty soon it's almost like hotdog night. Except it's different because they bought them big bottles a coke, so you can't have your own. And they have beer, so Daddy and Ma don't eat. And Ma tells the girls to feed the little kids. And it's not dark out. And the Lawn Ranger's not on TV, but Sky King is.

Mary tells Ma the ice cream melted in the car. Ma says not

to tell Daddy.

I say to Junior, "It took four of them to hold you down!"

He says, "You better not tell Daddy you went to get bread because he thinks you went to call the police and he already got mad about that. So don't go and make him mad about something else!"

I say, "I won't say nothing, Junior."

And then he shows me out the pitcher window where Missus Benet lives. He spits on the window and draws a little circle. Then he picks me up and puts my head right where his head was when he spit, and he says, "If you look at that spit mark you can see right where she lives."

So I was right—you just stay on this side of the road to get bread.

Sometimes Junior picks on us, but he's the best there is. But so is Jean. Yvonne is, too. And so is Charlotte. And so, well, they're all the best. Next time, I'll just go get bread when Junior says to and stop all that fighting.

CHAPTER 5

DE DEEDLE DE DE

When Daddy ain't talking to Ma, he lets you sit on his foot like it's a horsey. Then he grabs both your hands and lifts you way up with his foot, and he swings you up and down and up and down! And when he's doing that he starts singing like,

De deedle de de

De de de de

De deedle de de

De de!

No wait—De deedle de de—yeah that's right!

De deedle de

De de de de

De deedle de de

De de!

And that's lots of fun! But then the little kids start climbing on him because they want a ride, too. So you have to get off and take turns. But sometimes he does two at a time. That's even more fun! So the one in the back hangs on to the one in the front, like I get on first and then they help Gracey get on and hang on to me. And he goes, "de deedle de de de de de de," and we all get laughing, and Daddy laughs like he does when he's drinking beer and ain't mad at the jews.

But pretty soon he gets tired and says, "Now go on out and

play." We try to get him to do more, but he won't. So Ma says go out and play before he blows up. So we clear out.

When you go outside, everybody's doing something different. So you can pick what you like to do. Like Charlotte and Bev take these little stones and draw pictures on that big flat stone over by the house. And they make up stories. Like Charlotte draws a pretty girl on the stone and makes her have ribbons in her hair and says she's going to a party.

Then Bev says something about the girl, like, "She gets into the car!" So Charlotte draws that. Then they erase it and draw what happens next. They get mad if you walk across the stone. Or if you throw water on it, Bev chases you right around the house—and she punches hard. But you can sit and watch the stories if you don't say anything bad like that's the dumbest story ever.

Mary jumps rope all day or plays hopscotch with Pearl and Gracey. They draw all these boxes in the dirt. Then they have to jump where the stone lands. But they have to jump on one foot, so it's not easy. They let Gracey pretend jump because she's so little.

When Mary jumps rope, she sings a song about someone so they'll chase her. Like if you're a boy, she'll sing about you kissing some girl. And when you chase her, she keeps jumping rope and running at the same time. You never can catch her because she's got on that green dress that's good for running and them saddle shoes.

Johnny and me play cowboys, like the ones on TV. We go down by the apple tree, and he tells me what to do. But you have to pick who's the bad guy first, because he's the one that's gonna get shot or get pretend beat up, so nobody wants to be him. To pick the bad guy, you have to remember who was bad last, and then you just take turns.

Johnny says, "I was the bad guy over by the road!"

I say, "No sir! I was the bad guy upstairs!" And you fight like that for a while. But pretty soon you have to pick, or you never get to play.

So Johnny says, "It's like you robbed five banks, and you go into the bar for a drink, then you turn around and say, 'It's time to draw your gun, mister!'"

So I turn around and say, "It's time to draw your gun, mister!"

Then he says, "Okay, now you draw your gun, but I shoot it outta your hand."

So I draw my gun, but he's faster because he's good, and he shoots it right outta my hand! And—oh yeah—every time you shoot somebody, you make a clicking noise with your mouth, so it sounds like a real shot.

Then we get into a pretend fight, and he says, "You duck and hit me in the stomach!" So I do that, and he falls down.

Then he says, "Okay, now you come over and step on my head, but I grab your foot."

So I do that, and he grabs my foot and I fall down. Then he gets on top of me and pretends to punch me in the face. And every time he punches, he makes that clicking sound, so it seems real. It's really that same clicking noise he makes when he's shooting the gun, but it's good for punching, too.

He punches me until I say, "Okay, now I knock you off!" Then I swing a punch at his head, and he falls off. But sometimes he don't fall off like he's posta! So I call the big kids and they come and drag him off. Then we climb the apple tree and get into pretend fights up there like Tarzan and the lions. But we don't really fall.

We got this stick that looks something like the Rifleman's gun, so I use it for that. But Johnny uses it for a bat. He pretends he's playing baseball and picks up stones and bats them across the road, and I use it to shoot pretend Indians.

He says, "There's a man on first and Mickey's up to bat!" Then he flips the stone up in the air in front of him, and when it comes down he whacks it hard and hollers, "It's outta the park!" Or if he misses the stone he hollers, "Strike one!" And that's fun to watch.

Then I say, "Hey, I want to play with the gun."

And he says, "It ain't a gun, it's a bat."

"No! It's a gun!"

"No! It's a bat!"

And if Johnny knows you want it really bad, he won't ever give it to you. So the only way you can get it is if you go and find something that seems like more fun. Then he wants to do that too, and he drops the bat and forgets it. Then I run back and pick it up and holler, "Hardy-har-har! I told you it's a gun!" Then we play cowboys again, but we use our fingers instead of the bat because we just fight over the bat and don't ever get to play. I mean, we fight over the gun.

So here's how playing all day works. It's easier to play with the little kids because they just do what you tell them to do. But it's more fun to play with the big kids because they make you do things you don't really want to do and after a while that makes you not so afraid. So when you go to school and somebody knuckles you, you just knuckle them right back. Or you can trick them to be nice and play with you because you already did that with the big kids at home.

Being big and going to work like Daddy is hard, but playing all day is harder. At work you just do what they tell you, but at play you make up new rules every day so you don't get hurt. Sometimes it works, and sometimes it doesn't. But mosta the time, the big kids are there to catch you if you fall or if they throw you down.

Like one time we see Junior going across the road to climb the big tree. He climbs way up to the top and swings back and forth and screams out, "Hey everybody look at me!" and you see the tree going back and forth, but you can't see him because of all the leaves. So everybody runs across the road. Nobody can climb like Junior! But I will when I get big because Junior says you can see the whole world up there.

One other time we went over there and mosta the leaves was on the ground. Then we could see him up there really good. He hollers down, "Hey Fuzzy Head! Come on up!" But they won't let me climb. So he scoots down and starts to push all the leaves into this big ditch. We all help him and pretty soon we fill the ditch right up. Then the big kids all start jumping in!

So then Junior climbs this skinny tree and makes it bend right over the hole. He's hanging way up there screaming, "Help me! Help! I'm gonna fall!"

Jean hollers up at him, "Junior, you stop that right now."

Bev whispers to me, "It's okay—he's just pretending."

But I think that maybe he really is in trouble, so I holler out, "Hey Junior! Just drop right in them leaves!" So he lets go and drops right in. He goes right under the leaves and don't come up. That makes us all ascared.

Bev yells out, "I'm getting Ma and Daddy!" Then he pops up and scares us all! So we throw leaves at him.

Junior hollers at Johnny and me, "You jump off the bank!" And he shows us how to do it. Johnny jumps right in, but it's way too high for me. So Johnny calls me scaredy-cat.

Junior says, "Here you go, Fuzzy! I'll catch you!" But I'm not gonna do it.

Junior says to Bev, "You throw him off to me." So I run away from there. But they grab me and drag me back by the ditch. So I kick and scream and throw myself around. But pretty soon I get tired of that and I say, "Okay! I'll jump if you catch me."

Bev helps me jump, but when she lets me go, Junior jerks outta the way, and I fall way down under them leaves. At first, I start to cry, but when they dig me out I'm laughing because it was so much fun. So then I don't cry no more, and I make them throw me off again and again and again until they get tired like Daddy gets tired when he bounces you. Then they tell me to go and look for worms, but not down by where the Devil lives.

So then they take the little kids and throw them into the ditch, but only pretend. Like they take Gracey and Pearl and pass them around the ditch. Then they hand them down to the kids in the hole and go, "Look at them fly!" And everybody goes, "Weeeee! Weeeee!" in a real high voice like Ma does when she's changing Lori and makes her laugh and smile. They don't ever drop the little kids in the leaves because Jean won't let them. Like she gets way bossy about the little kids, specially Lori and Chuck.

Sometimes we fight out there, but mosta the time we don't. After a long time, Ma calls the girls to do the dishes, or Daddy calls Junior to help him work on the house. But when Daddy's drinking, he don't work, so then we stay outside mosta the day. Like who wants to go in there anyways? Daddy grabs your arm and makes you talk to him about his work or how he and his brothers punched the immagrits and made them walk on the other side of the street. Or sometimes he cries because his uncle Bill got his arm shot off in the civil war, but Ma says that's just the beer talking.

Even if you're little, you can play outside all by yourself. But you can't go too far from the house. And you can't start fires. And you have to stay away from where the Devil lives.

CHAPTER 6

JUSt SAY BOO!

One time I got so afraid I couldn't move.

Mary wouldn't do it, so the big kids told me to take the little kids outside so they could fight it out and the little kids don't hear. So I was standing out there watching them like I was posta, and like these goosebumps come all over me and stuck me in one place. Charlotte sees me out the window and comes running out.

She looks at me and says, "It's okay Frankie, just breathe!" But I don't want to crack, so I hold in my breath until it comes out slow through my skin. Charlotte shakes me and says to Yvonne, "Let's make him walk."

Yvonne whispers, "No, we got to talk him out."

So they start saying nice things to make me feel better, like, "We was only joking in there," and "No one's gonna take us away," and "They'll be home really soon," and "The school nurse ain't coming here," and "We won't fight with each other no more!"

But I wasn't ascared of none of that. It was the angels on top of the trees that scared me. They was growling, and they're posta be nice! And there was Russians crawling all through the woods. Not the kind that was on TV but real ones that spy on you when no one's looking and stab you! And there's too many of us, and I was gonna die like Chipper across the road, and then they would come home, and Daddy would be mean to Junior. And they made Jean be valatorian so she has to go to college.

Well, they all start hugging and tickling me to break me outta being stuck. Then they all get together and put me in a blanket and toss me way up in the air and make me laugh a lot. Then they take me inside and make me coffee with lots of cream and sugar because I'm almost big. Pretty soon Charlotte says she's gonna take me for a walk.

We're walking up the hill, and when we can't see the house no more, she stops and spins around and grabs my shoulders. She says, "Whatever it is you're ascared of, Frankie, I know it's real."

I say, "You mean the Russians?"

She says, "Yes! The Russians! They're real!"

I say, "They got these big long knives."

She says, "That's so they can stab you." And she pushes a pretend knife right through my head.

I say, "Are they really gonna do that?"

She says, "Well, we know they want to drop that bomb." Then she looks close at me and says, "Where was they anyways?"

I point and say, "They was crawling all through them woods."

She looks around and says, "Cripes Frankie! If you'd a told me I'd a brought a knife!"

I say, "Well, they went away when you was tickling me."

She says, "Well, never mind. Let's just get home before they come back." And she starts walking down the hill really fast. She gets way ahead of me and hollers back, "It's a good thing I know how to get rid of them!" So I run and catch up to her and pull on her dress and make her tell me how to do it.

She says, "It's easy to get rid of them, once you know where they start." Then she asks me where they start.

I say, "The angels was growling."

She says, "Oh, I figgered that. I mean where do they really start?"

I say, "I don't know."

She says, "Well think about it. Where do you see them first?"

So I think about it a long time, and then I point at my head.

She says, "That's right! They always start in your head before they creep down the woods or crawl under the bed. But that's what makes them so easy to get rid of."

I don't know what she means, so I say, "Let's just go home."

She says, "No! Wait just a minute."

Then she wraps her fingers around my head and uses her thumbs to close my eyes. She hollers out so I can hear, "Okay now, call a Russian up!"

I tell her I can't do that with her thumbs in my eyes, but she shakes my head and says she ain't going nowhere until I call a Russian up. She says, "Not all of them, just one or two."

So pretty soon I see one. He's big and scary and has a knife to cut me open. I tell her I can see one, sort of. She tells me to look until I can see him real good.

When I do that, I shake my head like saying yes.

Then she says, "Okay, now make him smaller." I tell her I can't do that, and she says it's my head and I can do what I want with what's inside. She says, "You made him big and scary, now make him tiny, like a mouse. Like small enough to fit in your hand."

Well, that worked pretty good! And pretty soon I see them Russians in the woods again, but they was small so I could step on them like worms, and that made me happy. Charlotte says she draws her monsters on the flat stone and when she erases them, sometimes they go away for good.

I like Charlotte because she's like Ma, but so is Jean. I tell her the Russians are scary because it seems like they want you to die like Chipper. She says, "Yeah, that's what makes them such monsters."

I ask her if they're really gonna drop that bomb because the big kids told me they was pretend hiding from it under the desks at school. She said the president was old and bald, but he kicked the Nazis in the war, and he can kick the Russians, too.

Then she says there's one more thing I can do after I make the Russians really small. She says to just point at them and holler "Boo! Boo!" So then we run all the way home hollering Boo! Boo-boo-boo! Boo-boo-boo! And that was really fun. Boo-boo-boo! Ha-ha-ha! All you dumb old monsters. So who's ascared now?

CHAPTER 7

WHERE +HE DEVIL LIVES

The Devil's down the road by where the bus picks up the kids for school. He's right by where you go if you don't go all the way to Missus Benet's house. It's a dirt road, so when the cars go by, dust gets in your mouth and you take your shirt off to wipe your tongue. Well, that's where the Devil is.

One day, we're all down there playing by where the bus stops—right by that old barn that's falling down. We ain't posta go in there because Daddy says it'll fall on you. But the big kids go in there when it's windy or snowy or rainy and the bus is late. They don't tell Daddy they went in there because Ma says he might kill them instead of the barn killing them. But she was just being funny—ha-ha!

Well, this one day we're all down there, and Johnny and Junior are throwing stones at birds and looking for snakes and picking them green apples across the road. And the girls are playing freeze tag. Except Bev's watching Pearl and Gracey. I'm turning over rocks and stones to see what jumps out, like a bug or a worm or something else to step on.

Anyways, this one rock has a hole under it, so I start to dig down the hole to see what's there. I can't see nothing, so I lay on my belly and try to look down the hole. Right then is when I hear this noise down there. So I call out, "There's something down there, Bev!"

I grab a stick and start digging down real fast. But she comes over and says, "You better put that rock right back on that hole, mister!"

I say, "Why, Bev?"

She says, "I thought you said you heard something move down there."

I say, "I did."

She says, "Well, can't you even guess who it is?"

"You mean like a woodchuck?"

She says, "Don't you even know where the Devil lives?"

"He lives way down in the ground!"

She says, "Where do you think he comes up?"

"I don't know."

She says, "Well, where do you think he gets his air?"

"I don't know!"

"Well, put your eye down there again and then you'll know!" So I lay on my belly and put my eye right over the hole.

She says, "Can you see anything, Frankie?"

"It's way too dark!"

"Well, can you hear anything?" So I put my ear over the hole.

I say, "No, I don't hear nothing."

"You got to listen real good!" So I do that, but I still don't hear nothing.

She says, "If you close your eyes you can hear better." So I do that and listen real good. And pretty soon I hear this scraping noise.

I holler, "It sounds like someone's down there moving rocks!"

She says, "Cripes! That's what the Devil does all day long."

So I jump back. "Well, maybe it's a snake!"

She says, "Everybody knows the Devil turns into a snake—he did that in the Bible!"

I say, "Oh, yeah!" Like when Adam and Eve ate that apple and got bare naked because the Devil tricked them.

So Bev puts her ear down by the hole and listens real good too.

She whispers, "It sounds like maybe he's looking for worms to eat."

I say, "Well, I just stepped on some worms."

She looks up at me. "What! Are you trying to get him mad?"

So I say, "Let's go get Jean."

She says, "No, because he'll just go and hide from her."

"Then let's put sticks down that hole." But she says that will only make the Devil mad.

So I say, "What are we gonna do?"

She says, "Why don't we just put the rock back real quiet, and he'll never even know we was here." So we put the rock back where it was.

Then she says, "Okay now, here's the rules. You can't tell nobody you know where the Devil lives or he'll get mad at you. And you can't ever come down here by yourself because then he might eat you up! And don't step on any more worms because they might be his food."

Then she makes me tell the rules back to her and cross my heart and hope to die.

When we was all going back up the road, I say to Bev, "Why is the Devil so afraid of Jean?" She laughs and says he ain't afraid of her, he just don't like too many big people knowing he's there because then he can't trick the little kids and make them do bad things.

I say, "Well, maybe Jean will make the Devil go away for good."

She says, "The Devil don't usually go away." I ask her what would make him go?

She says, "You have to read the Bible every day and pray and go to church." But I don't like that because Daddy says he'll cut your throat if you pray at the table, and he don't like us to go to church because he don't like us ramming all over them hills. And I don't like church anyways. They just talk all day and make you sit there and be quiet like you did something bad.

I say, "Bev, will you read me the Bible?"

She says just telling Bible stories is good enough. So I don't really have to be ascared, because the big girls tell lots of Bible stories at night and that makes it so the Devil don't come upstairs to get us.

We're walking up the hill and Bev's carrying Gracey on her back and I'm pulling Pearl, and I say, "It's too bad you can't kill worms but you can kill birds."

Bev says, "Well, it ain't good to kill birds, Frankie." But she says that's for a different reason. It's because God likes to watch the birds fly around and play, the same as people likes to watch them. She says that's why God made birds in the first place, so he can have fun watching them.

I say, "Well, you better tell Junior and Johnny that because they was throwing stones at the birds before."

She says, "Did you ever see them hit one?"

I say, "No."

She says, "That's because God gives them extra puffs of air so they can fly away in time." So that's how God takes care of the little birds. But I sure wish he'd step on that Devil!

CHAPTER 8

NIGHtY-NIGHt

When we go to bed, it's dark. I mean, there ain't no lights upstairs like there is downstairs, because Daddy's still building the house. But the big kids carry lights up there, so you can see okay to go to bed. Like Jean takes a light into her room. But it shines into our room because the walls ain't there yet. Except for them boards that go up and down. It's fun to walk through them walls and be like ghosts!

They make the little kids go to bed first, the boys in one and girls in the other. And they tell us go right to sleep. But Johnny puts his feet in your face, or Gracey keeps talking over there about nothing. Sometimes Pearl and her sing dumb songs like, "My Bonnie Lies Over the Ocean," or "Row, Row, Row Your Boat." So how can you sleep?

Then Ma comes in and says a prayer over us, like, "Now I Lay Me Down to Sleep." Or sometimes she makes us say it. Or she'll sing a song from when she was a little girl going to church like, "On a hill far away was this old rugged cross." But singing like that makes her cry, so I like it better when she prays. On the way down, she tells us to cover up our ears or we'll all go deaf.

When we close our eyes, we can hear the big kids downstairs having all the fun. So we tell Pearl and Gracey to get outta their bed and holler down that we need a drink. But they holler back up for us to go to bed because they know we ain't really thirsty. Junior hollers up, "It'll make you pee your pants!" Then everybody down there laughs, like that's even funny.

Sometimes they make popcorn on the stove, and you can hear it popping and the smell makes you hungry. If you cry enough, they bring you some. But then you really do get thirsty. Gracey's the best at crying to get things for us because when she cries, she thinks she really means it.

The most fun is when the big kids go to bed and you're still awake. Then we tell stories about what we did that day. Like Jean hollers over, "Hey Frankie, what did you do today?"

I say, "I don't even know." And everybody laughs.

"You mean you don't know what you did today?"

"I don't even know." And everybody laughs again.

So Junior says, "Well, did you get up this morning?"

"I don't even know." And everybody laughs again.

He says, "Well, did you put on Daddy's underwear?"

"I don't even know." And that makes everybody laugh real hard.

Then Charlotte says, "Hey Frankie, did you pick Missus Benet's nose?"

And I keep saying, "I don't even know."

And they keep asking dumb things like, "Did you pull down your pants and slide on the ice?" or "Did you dig a hole to China?"

Then someone says a poem like, "Here's a penny, go kiss Jack Benny," or "You want a nickel? Go suck a pickle." And that makes everybody laugh. Or the big kids make one up. Like Charlotte says a poem about Daddy going bald.

One time Junior asks me, "What are you gonna say to

Missus Gaylord your first day of school?"

"I don't know."

He says, "You walk right up to her and holler 'Ain't!' That'll knock her right over."

I say, "No, I'm gonna walk right up to her and say 'Poopy!' And that'll knock her right over."

Charlotte says, "No—you go up to her and say 'Hey old lady, how about a beer!'"

So then Johnny says, "No, you go up to her and say 'How did you get so old and stupid?'"

Then Jean hollers out, "Now, you all knock that off!"

Junior says, "Well, he probably will make us look stupid."

Yvonne says, "No he won't! He's a good boy!"

I say, "I'll be really nice to Missus Gaylord."

Johnny says, "Well, what if she ain't nice to you?"

I say, "She just better be!" But I was getting ascared. Jean hollers over that she had Missus Gaylord when she was little, and she was always nice to the ones who did what she said. Junior says he remembers she was a battle-axe. Then he tells me to just make sure she keeps her big nose outta our business.

There ain't no way to remember all what we say at night because sometimes everybody gets talking and laughing at the same time. But pretty soon they start falling off to sleep one at a time. It's like turning down the radio real slow. And then you just wake up.

One time I sat up and bumped my head on the bed because I was under it. And so was all the little kids! We was all covered up, but we was under the bed.

I go to the big kids, "Why did you go and do that?"

Charlotte says, "It was just for a joke."

But Johnny says he heard Daddy hollering when he came home last night. So I ask him if Daddy was drinking likker, and he says he don't know. But sometimes Daddy hollers like that when he's been drinking likker because it makes him crazy, and Ma says to hide the guns. Pearl says she heard Daddy make all the big kids get outta bed to talk to him. I asked her if he was mad at them, and she says no, he was mad at the president because when Daddy was a little boy, his big brother got killed in the war.

I tell them, "When I woke up in the middle of the night, I saw all these big feet running around the room, but I didn't know I was under the bed!" So we all laughed at that. Like how can big feet just be running around all by themselves? When I saw them feet I thought they was ghosts. But you don't tell nobody that, or they'll think you're crazy. Or drinking likker. Ha-ha-ha!

CHAPTER 9

You Just Get a Bowl

Before you go to school on the first day, you have to get a haircut, or they'll think you're really poor. Like Johnny Gray cuts Daddy's hair, and Daddy gives him money because he's the sheriff, too. But he don't wear a gun when he's cutting hair. Well, if Johnny Gray cuts your hair, you can't be poor because you got money to give him.

Jean cuts the little kids' hair because mosta the time we don't go to town anyways. And even if we do go to town, it's okay if she cuts your hair. That don't mean we're poor. It's because we're only little that she cuts our hair. Because if you're only little, it don't really matter how you look.

Well, this one night Ma tells Jean to cut my hair because I'm gonna go to kindygarden. But Jean says she's got way too much to do to get ready for school, so she ain't gonna do it.

Ma says, "You got to! His hair's sticking straight up!"

Jean says, "Why do I have to do everything?"

Ma says, "Now you can just cut his hair."

I say, "I don't want to look poor!" Ma didn't hear me, but Daddy did. So he gets mad and swears and hollers, "I'll cut his gaddam hair!"

Ma says, "Jean can do it better."

Daddy says, "What are you talking about? My father used

to cut my hair all the time!"

Ma goes, "Well, way back then everybody got their hair cut at home."

Daddy says, "It ain't no different now—you just get a gaddam bowl!"

But I don't want a bowl on my head because then everyone will laugh at me. So I holler, "No!"

But Daddy grabs a stool and puts me on it, and Johnny starts to laugh like I knew he would. I start to wiggle away, but Daddy grabs me and puts me back up there. Johnny points at me and laughs, but he's hiding behind the stove so Daddy can't see him.

So I point and yell out, "Johnny's laughing at me!"

Daddy spins around and hollers, "I'll break his fecking neck!" So Johnny runs away from there.

Then Daddy tells me to take off my shirt, but it's way too cold, so I say, "No!" Daddy tells Ma to make me mind, so she comes over and takes off my shirt. Then Daddy gets this bowl that Ma makes bread in, but that's too big and everybody laughs. So I get mad and climb off the chair, but Daddy puts me right back on.

He hollers down, "Now you just sit there, mister!"

So they get a bowl that fits my head better, but it's really cold without my shirt, so I start to shake. And Daddy says for me to hold still. But the bowl's cold too, so I start shaking more. So Daddy holds onto my neck, and he starts cutting my hair with these big scissors. But every time he snips by my ears, I jump. That makes Daddy madder and he hollers at me, "Don't act like such a baby!"

It gets worse after that. I don't have on no shirt, and hair's falling down my neck and making me itch and scratch, and it's cold there by the stove except the part of you that's right next to it. I was crying, but just a little because he hollered at me again, and he was hurting my neck where he was trying to hold me still.

Pretty soon Ma says, "Look here, Elmer. You're going way too short!"

He says, "Well, make him hold still!" But I kept wiggling.

So Daddy grabs me hard, and I yell, "You stop hurting my neck!" But he don't stop, so that makes me cry more. I mean, what if someone hurt your neck? So I try to get down, but he makes me stay there, and now all the kids come in to watch because I'm fighting Daddy. But I'm not really fighting him— I'm just trying to get down. So he starts swearing at me and everybody else.

So then Ma says, "Why don't you let Jean take over?" But he won't because he thinks he can do it better like his daddy did when he was little like me.

So Ma says, "Now take that bowl off his head because this part don't match that part."

I go, "Ma! It does too match! Make him stop!" So Daddy knocks the bowl off my head and tells me to straighten up and act like a man.

So I say, "You stop hurting my neck, mister!"

He says when he was little, he never jumped around like that or his daddy would've knocked him right off the chair.

So I say, "You should've punched him!" But he didn't hear me good because I was crying and sniffing way too hard.

So he throws down the scissors and hollers, "You get outta my sight!"

Ma says, "Oh, Elmer."

He says, "Afraid of a bowl!"

Ma says, "Now he's got nicks all over his head."

I see Junior over by the door watching me cry. He puts both hands on his head and runs upstairs. But why's he mad at me? I seen him cry before—even when he was big—like that time the big girls held him down.

So I holler at him, "Yeah, well Johnny Gray cuts your hair!" But I was crying too much to get it out right. Now Johnny looks at me, but he ain't laughing like before. Then Daddy yells at me to go to bed.

So someone takes me up the stairs and puts me into bed. Jean comes over and looks at me, and says, "Oh, my goodness!" Then she goes, "He's got hair all over himself—he can't sleep like that." I'm trying to stop crying, but I'm still shaking way too hard.

So then Jean gets mad at Daddy, and she goes over to the stairs and hollers down at him, "Like you're so tough, mister!" And then she comes over by the bed and looks at me again, and then she goes back over by the stairs and hollers down, "Did you ever think of picking on somebody your own size?" But Daddy was just trying to cut my hair like his daddy cut his, so he wasn't really picking on me like she says.

Or maybe it was Yvonne that hollered down about Daddy picking on me. But I think it was Jean, because when she gets mad she stands there and hollers at Daddy, even if she's ascared. But Yvonne cries and runs away.

Daddy hollers something back at Jean so she screams down, "You spent all your money going out, or he could've gone to Johnny Gray's!" Then Daddy hollers up them really bad words, but he gets quiet after that.

So then Jean starts crying. It's crying like Ma does when she sings them church songs at night. It ain't loud like when the little kids cry, but quiet so you have to look to see it. I try to reach up and give her a hug, but I'm still shaking way too much.

I say, "I'm gonna tell Johnny Gray because he's got a gun." Junior's walking around the room punching at the air, just like me and Johnny do when we pretend to fight bad guys.

I say, "Well, why is he mad at me?"

They say, "He ain't mad at you, Frankie—he was just trying to cut your hair." But I meant, why is Junior mad at me—not Daddy.

Then Johnny comes over by the bed, and he says, "You was really brave to fight him like that." But I wasn't fighting nobody. I was only trying to get down off the chair.

Jean says to Junior, "Don't you say a word to him because he'll come after you!" But he don't dare come after Jean.

Junior says, "I ain't afraid a nobody!" He keeps punching at the air and that's when I figger out Junior's mad at Daddy and not mad at me, so right then I stop crying.

Then Jean tells Bev to sneak down and get a wet towel to wash the hair off of me.

Bev says, "He's right there smoking by the stove. How am I gonna heat the towel up?"

Jean says, "It's okay, because he ain't mad at you."

And Bev says, "No, but he sure is mad!"

But I tell them not to wash me off because that's too cold.

So Jean says, "Well, okay, but how are you gonna sleep with all them tickly-wicklies?" And they all start tickling me, so I start laughing.

Then Bev and Charlotte start fighting over who's gonna wear the blue skirt, so everything's the same as it was before I got my hair cut. And that's what makes you tired, because when you feel bad you can't sleep. But when you feel good, you can't even keep your eyes open.

Well, I'm going off to sleep and I hear Junior say, "That's just a great way for him to start school."

Mary comes over to me and says, "What's Missus Gaylord going to say?"

But Jean says she can fix me up after I go to sleep, and she'll wash me off, too. She says that's the last time Daddy cuts anybody's hair in this house.

I'm dropping off to sleep. It seems like everybody's floating right above me and that feels really good because they're on my side. They're saying how good I am and how I ain't a baby like Daddy said. And Junior says I ain't a Fuzzy Head no more. I try to tell Johnny I was only trying to get down, but I'm way too tired to say it.

When I wake up, I'm all washed off and most of my hair is fixed. So that's good. I wake up Pearl and tell her when I get big I won't ever let Daddy punch Junior because he was gonna go fight for me last night but Jean told him not to.

Johnny comes over and says, "I would've hold still better."

Jean hollers in to Johnny, "Held! I would've held still!" She likes us to talk right, like all them teachers do at school, because she's gonna be a teacher, too. But Missus Gaylord's only kindygarden, so you can talk bad until she teaches you to talk right. Except you can't ever swear like Daddy does. Like you don't ever say, "You just get a gaddam bowl." You say, "You just get a bowl." Then Missus Gaylord will be nice to you.

CHAPTER 10

GEttING DADDY OUt

Daddy's always the first one up, and he gets up way early. But Ma don't want to get up right then, so she stays in bed. But Daddy wants her to get up so he can talk to her. So he hollers upstairs, "Hey, Mary! Get outta bed!" Then he goes back down and you can hear him whistling and putting on wood. Then he goes way down cellar and puts on coal, and you can hear him whistling and shoveling down there, if the fire ain't too low. If it's too low, he swears and says he's getting a new one that burns oil.

It seems like he's talking to the stove, but he really ain't. Junior's still in bed, and he pretends he's the stove talking back to Daddy. But he says it really low so Daddy can't hear him.

Like he says, "Oh, no! Don't get rid of me! I been a good stove!" Then he pretends he's the stove crying, and everybody who's awake gets laughing. Then Junior says to the little kids, "Don't you go and tell Daddy I said that, because he'll get mad at you."

To help Junior, I say to them, "Yeah, and then Daddy'll make you keep the fire going in the middle of the night!" And Johnny tells them Daddy'll make them eat coal for breakfast. And we say funny things like that. We know they ain't really true things, but it makes the little kids act right so Daddy don't get mad at Junior.

Coal can be good or bad. I mean Santa brings you coal for Christmas if you're bad. But Bev says you have to be bad all the time, and no one is, except the Devil. One time when I was real little they rubbed orange lipstick on my face and took me around for Halloween and Missus Benet gave me some apples. She says we come out way too early or she would have had candy. But I like them apples because she buys them at the store.

Well, she gives me the whole bowl, so I take it and start out the door. But they make me bring the bowl back, and Bev says, "You only take one, Frankie!" But Missus Benet laughs and gives me two apples anyways. So I got two. But then Mary eats one of them when I ain't looking! I tell Ma later, but she lets her get away with it because Mary likes apples better than anybody.

When Ma don't get right up, Daddy comes to the bottom of the stairs again, and hollers out, "Hey Mary get outta bed!" Or he hollers, "Lazy Mary get outta bed! We need the sheets for the table!" He's only joking about them sheets. He likes to tell stories about people doing dumb things like that. Like dogs licking off your plates. Or people's pants falling down.

If Ma don't get right up, he brings her up a cup of coffee and says, "Here now, your coffee's getting cold." So she gets up to make him breakfast. Then they talk about things that everybody has to do that day. Like Daddy tells her what he wants the big kids to do. He says that Junior has to take rocks outta the cellar and put them in a ditch or on the truck. Or he says, "Make Johnny bring in some wood after school."

Sometimes Junior says back, "I ain't your slave." But Daddy don't hear him because Junior's still in bed.

Then Daddy tells Ma to do something like, "You clear that stuff outta the big room so I can nail them boards up when I get home."

Ma says back, "Well, I cleared it out for you before, but you didn't get to it, and the kids filled it right back up!"

Daddy says, "Well, I had to get the garden ready!"

Ma says, "Of course you did." Then Daddy goes to work. But first we have to find his stuff.

He says, "Hey Mary, grab me some socks!"

Ma answers back, "You know where the sock drawer is!"

He says, "Well go and get me some!"

Ma goes, "Just go and dig them out!"

He says, "You're gonna make me late!"

She says, "I have to feed the little kids!"

So he tells Yvonne, "Go get me some socks!" So she goes to the sock drawer and finds him socks. Ma says, "Make sure they match, and don't grab the girls' socks because he don't even look at what you give him."

Then we have to find his hat. He wears one of them hats for carpenters. Ma says he won't go to work without a hat because all his hair is falling out. She says things like that right in front of him and he don't even hear!

I pull on Ma's dress and whisper up, "Ma! He's gonna hear!"

She says, "Don't you dare tell him I said that."

Daddy says, "What did you say, Mary?"

Ma says, "Oh, nothing, Elmer." So I run right outta there!

Daddy don't get mad about his hat, unless we can't find it before Vern comes to pick him up. Then he starts hollering, "Which one of you was playing with my hat!" So that makes everybody look.

Ma tells someone, "You scoot upstairs and see if it's by the bed." So someone scoots up there. Or you can look under the couch or behind the stove, or on the pile a wood, or where we put the coats or in the crib, or anyplace else, because maybe the kids really did leave it someplace, just like Daddy said. Pearl and Gracey like to wear his hat playing carpenters. That makes Daddy laugh. He rubs their heads and says, "Ain't you cute," because girls can't be carpenters.

Well, if you find his hat, you holler out, "Right here it is!" Then we give it to Ma and she gives it to Daddy and then he takes it from her and slaps it against his leg and puts it on his head.

Ma says, "Well, thank you too, sir!"

But she ain't really thanking him. When she says 'thank you' like that, she really means, "Hey mister, the kids found your hat, and I give it to you, but you didn't even say thank you!" It's like Ma talks two ways to Daddy. But Daddy don't get what she really means, because he only talks one way. It's like when he says something, he means it just like he says it, but Ma might mean the same thing two ways. So you have to listen real good when she talks to know what she really means.

Then Ma gives him his lunch to get him out the door before Vern comes in. If Vern comes in and sits at the table, you have to give him coffee before they go to work. Giving coffee is good, but that makes Vern talk too much, and then Daddy gets late for work.

Like Vern says, "Hey Elmer, don't you think we need more rain?"

And Daddy says, "What do you mean? It's still too wet to plow the garden."

And Vern says, "What?" Because he's almost deaf.

And Daddy says, "It's too wet to plow!"

And Vern says back, "Sure I'll help you plow."

So Daddy hollers loud, "No! It's too wet to plow!"

And Vern says, "It's too damn wet, ain't it, Elmer."

So Daddy says to Ma, "He's getting worse."

And Ma says, "He's deaf as a post."

So I say, "How can a post be deaf, Ma?"

She whispers back, "Don't say that so loud or he might hear you."

So I say, "How can he hear if he's deaf as a post?"

And she says, "It's just a way of talking, Frankie."

Then she tells me to tell Daddy it's time to go to work, but not to let Vern hear because that's rude. So I go in and say to Daddy real quiet, "Hey Daddy, Ma says it's time to go to work." But he don't hear me. So I pull on his arm and tell him again.

He says, "Go put my tools by the door."

Vern's still drinking coffee, so none of the girls want to eat at the table because he's sitting in there. So they tell me to go get Vern and Daddy out the door. So I take Daddy's hat and put it back on his head.

Ma says, "Here's your hat Elmer, what's your hurry?" But Daddy and Vern don't hear that because she's just being funny for the big kids. They're all piling up in the kitchen, fixing their food and washing up and waiting for the table to get cleared of Vern and Daddy.

Ma tells them, "From now on we have to get your daddy out before Vern comes in." But we never do. So Ma goes in to wash off the table, and she puts plates down for the kids to eat, but Vern still don't get that she wants him out.

So Ma points at her wrist and says, "Hey Vern, what time is it?"

And he looks at his watch and says, "Dam Elmer, we have to go!"

Then Daddy stands up and says, "Where did you put my tools, Frankie?"

I say, "They're over by the door."

Then they start to go outside. Ma says, "Don't forget your lunch bucket!" She always puts in two cupcakes, but he don't ever eat them. Ma says he just wants them in his lunch bucket so he looks like he's got money enough to buy food he don't even eat. So when he gets home, the little kids fight over who's gonna get them cupcakes. Well, sometimes I fight over them, too.

When they get out the door, Ma pushes it shut. Then she lays back against it and says, "Thank God!" But she really ain't thanking God—she's just glad we got them two out the door. So when she says "Thank God!" she's just talking two ways like she does. It's okay for her to talk two ways, mosta the time. But when she does it to God like that, how does she know he ain't gonna get mad because she ain't really thanking him and he knows everything?

So I say, "Ma, God's gonna hear you!" But she doesn't say nothing back because now she's got to get the big kids out. Bev says God likes you to thank him even if you don't really mean it because that's better than nothing, and nobody ever thanks God. Well, we would thank God for food, but Daddy don't let us pray at the table. But sometimes we sneak one in when he ain't looking.

So I say to Pearl, "Well, I got Daddy and Vern out, and I really, really, really do thank God for that!"

CHAPTER 11

HERE COMES THE BUS!

Mary can jump four stairs at a time! But I'll tell that later. When you're telling about the bus coming, you have to tell about things one at a time, which ain't so easy. So much is going on when the big kids try to make the bus, it would be lots better to tell it all at once or show it on TV.

Like when we try to get Vern and Daddy out, the big kids is running around the kitchen and upstairs, getting ready for school as much as they can. When Daddy goes out, everybody runs in by the big table and starts gobbling down what Ma's cooking.

Ma's feeding the little kids at the same time, because they got to eat as soon as they get up. But I like to wait until Daddy goes to work so I can have cocoa and toast. Well, I can have cocoa and toast when he's home, but he don't like no one to dunk toast. He says it ain't right to dunk toast because it makes a big mess, and you have to suck it up like a pig. And he says drinking too much cocoa puts a hole in your liver.

But Ma makes toast really good! Like she takes a bunch of bread and puts it on the stove where it ain't too hot. Then she turns it over when it gets brown just right. Then she puts butter on it, or jelly. But I never have jelly on toast because you can't dunk right with jelly. And jelly makes your fingers sticky. And besides, cocoa don't go good with jelly.

You just fold up the toast after you put butter on it. Then you dip it right in the cocoa and suck it in your mouth like a pig. That's what makes it taste so good! Ma says I'm the only one that eats four toasts. And if you wait until Daddy goes to work, you can sit at the big table to eat. If you don't fight, you can stay right there all morning because nobody even sees you when they're running around getting ready for school.

Pretty soon Ma hollers out, "The bus will be here any minute!" So everybody starts eating and washing and running around looking for school clothes real fast. Ma knows where everything is, so she tells them where to look.

Like she says to Johnny, "Your pants is in the clothes basket by the couch!" Or, she tells Bev her bobby pins is on the ice box, or who took the hairbrush upstairs and where they put it. Or if the big kids is fighting, she tells them to knock it off.

The big kids ain't afraid of Ma, but mosta the time they do what she says because they don't want her to feel bad. And she cries if she has to get mean. Like when she says she's gonna spank someone, she starts crying. Then they do what she says, but not because they might get spanked. It's because when Ma cries, everybody goes to school feeling bad.

Or sometimes Ma makes them mind her by saying, "I'll tell your father when he gets home!" She don't ever tell him, but she says that anyways.

Like she says, "If you miss the bus, your father's gonna hear about it!" But she don't ever tell him because he gets way too mad and that's worse than kids missing the bus. Like he hollers how he's gonna cut your throat or knock off your head. Or he might break something Ma likes.

So anyways, Ma hollers out, "Whoever's ready, watch for the bus!" So Junior or someone stands by the pitcher window and looks way up the road where you can see the bus come by Missus Gashay's house. Then whoever's watching hollers out, "Here comes the bus!" And everybody screams, like, "Where's my coat?" or "Where did you put my books?" or "Don't forget your glasses!"

And they get running around like wild horses. Then whoever's watching for the bus hollers out, "Not really!" Then they all get mad at him and call him names and go back upstairs laughing. Then everything starts to go slower again. Ma stands by the door with a washcloth, so she can grab you in case you missed a spot. Sometimes she washes you even if you ain't going to school—and she rubs way too hard!

She says, "Well, I have to get that spot!"

When it was my turn to go to school, Ma was washing my face, and Junior says to Ma, "Make him wear a hat."

I say, "You don't have no hat on!"

He says, "Well, Daddy didn't cut my hair!"

I say, "Well, Jean fixed my hair!"

He says back, "You just can't see the back of your head!"

I say, "I can too!"

Then Ma says, "You leave him alone."

And Junior says, "Then make him take another bus."

I say, "There ain't no other bus!"

Junior says, "Yeah, that's what I mean!"

Ma says, "He don't look so bad."

Then she says to me, "You're the cutest wittle fing!" And she pinches my cheek. But that's only for babies, so I pull her down to me and tell her not to say that in front of Junior.

Junior says, "The girls will sure be all over him."

I say, "I ain't playing with no girls!"

Junior says, "You got that right, Fuzzy Head!"

Ma says she's gonna slap him if he don't knock it off. Well, that makes her cry like she does because she likes Junior best. So I run over to punch Junior, but I see how he looks sad now too because he don't want to make Ma cry, like I said.

So instead of hitting him, I say, "I'm gonna be good at school, Junior. And Missus Gaylord's gonna like me!" Then I dance in little circles to make them laugh.

He says, "Well, she better or I'll come in and tip her over." I run over and grab Daddy's old hat and tell Junior I'm gonna wear it.

He laughs and takes it off and says, "No you ain't because that'll look worse!" Then he bends down and says, "Hey Fuzzy Head. You know the difference between a good haircut and a bad haircut?"

I say, "No."

He rubs my head and says, "Three days!" I don't get it, but I laugh anyways because now he's being nice to me. His hair looks really nice, and he says he can make my hair look just like his hair when I get big. Because mine sticks up like a rooster— only not just in the back.

The girls are mostly upstairs because they take longer to get ready. But then the bus really does come. So someone hollers out, "Here really really really comes the bus!" And they all come clomping down the stairs. That's when Mary jumps four steps and her dress goes right up over her head, and when she lands she keeps right on running for the door.

Ma hollers out, "Now you all get going!" Then we run by

her and push out the door—unless she grabs someone for the washcloth. We have to run all the way down the road by where the old barn is, and we have to beat the bus down there or the bus driver gets mad.

Way before I had to go to school, I was watching them all running down the road. I'm hollering out to Ma how everyone's making the bus or missing it.

I holler out, "Hey Ma! Junior's way ahead!"

She says, "Did Johnny get out the door yet?" Because he always tries to miss the bus.

I go, "Yeah! He's just going around the corner!"

She says, "Oh, God! Bev forgot her books!"

I say back, "No! She's coming back for them!"

It was funner to watch them running down the road before I had to go to school. Now it ain't no fun at all. When you see the bus coming down the road by Missus Gashay's, you have to run fast enough to beat it down by where it stops so the big kids don't get mad at you and the bus driver don't get mad, neither.

One time I'm running down the road with Bev, and my pants is falling down because my suspenders popped off.

She says, "Here! I'll carry your stuff! You just fix your pants!"

I'm running along pulling up my pants, and Bev's laughing but I'm crying and the bus is almost there, and every time I fix my suspenders they go popping off again and the other kids is hollering for us to hurry up and get down there!

When we come around the corner by where the Devil is, everybody's laughing and calling out like we're running a race! So I get laughing, too, and when the bus pulls up to load us on, I go running right past the big kids and jump right on the bus. And all the bus kids cheer like I won the race and the bus driver stands up and hollers, "Now that's how you be on time for the bus!"

But mosta the time it ain't like that. I mean, we make it down one at a time and the bus driver gets mad because when one gets on the bus, another one just breaks outta the house. The bus driver says, "It takes two and a half minutes to run down that dam hill, and I can't wait that long for every dam kid!" Sometimes the big kids tell him he's got to wait, and then he gets even madder.

One time he starts yelling at me because I was the last one down, so Jean steps in and says, "You just leave him alone and drive that bus, mister!" So he gets mad at her and jumps outta his seat and spins around like he's gonna hit her. But he's old and his teeth is fake, so they pop right outta his mouth and they hit the floor by my feet.

So I go over to pick them up—but they was all yucky! So when the bus kids see me grab them spitty teeth, they all go, "OOOOH!" He grabs his teeth, sucks them back into his mouth and sits down and starts swearing like Daddy does when he's mad. Jean tells him if he keeps that up, she'll tell Mister Klump.

He waves his arms and says to her, "Okay, now everybody just calm down!" Then he starts driving the bus like Jean told him to in the first place. Then all the bus kids start singing Elvis songs.

Sometimes we do get down there on time, but that ain't fun, either. Then you have to go by the big kids' rules for waiting for the bus. Like you can't stand in a straight line because that makes you look like the army and the bus kids might laugh. Or you can't get on in order, like the biggest to the littlest, because that looks really stupid. So you just have to stand there like having so many kids in one family ain't such a big deal. When the bus door opens, you just get on whenever you want, and you try not to be ascared.

Playing 'here comes the bus' used to be fun, before they made me go to school. But I don't like it for real because nothing ever goes right for all the kids at one time. And if Ma and Daddy don't come home the night before, or the night before that or the night before that, it seems like you ain't even posta go to school. But Jean makes us go. Then when you look back up the road, Ma ain't in the pitcher window looking out at us, and you can't even wave to her.

One time before I had to go to school, I'm by the pitcher window yelling to Ma how everybody's running down the road. She laughs and says, "You sound like you're calling out a horse race!" Then she comes over to the window by me and watches them make the bus.

She says, "God, I love them kids!"

You can tell by the way she says it she ain't talking two ways. So I go over and give her a hug by where the new baby is under that big dress. I say, "I do too, Ma."

She says, "Pretty soon you'll be going to school, Frankie."

I say, "No, Ma, I'm gonna stay home with you."

She says, "Oh God forbid!" I don't think God's mad at her for saying that because that time she wasn't talking two ways. I mean, I don't think she was.

CHAPTER 12

HOW MANY YOU HAVE

Missus Gaylord stands up there and hollers, "Children! It's time for us to get to know each other." Then she tells us to go around the room and say what our ma does and what our daddy does and how many you have.

So the kids go like, "My daddy works at the post office and ma takes care of the kids." Then they say how many brothers and sisters they have and who they are. Like they say, "I have two brothers and they're George and Joe."

Then Missus Gaylord says, "Very good, Susie!" Then she goes to the next one. But when it comes to me, I don't want to say nothing because Junior told me not to say anything stupid. So I sit there until Missus Gaylord makes me talk.

She says, "Just tell the class what your daddy does." But I don't talk. So she says I have to take a turn or she won't go on to the next one—and the next one's a girl so she was raising both hands to talk.

So I just whisper, "He's a carpenter."

She says, "What's that? A carpenter? Is your daddy a carpenter?"

I go, "I said he's a carpenter."

She says, "That's very good, Frankie!" Then she says to tell what Ma does. I say she takes care of the kids—like what does she think? Then she says to tell how many I have.

I ain't gonna say nothing about that, but she keeps waiting, so I say, "I got enough."

She says, "Yes Frankie, but how many?"

I say, "Well, Ma's gonna have a baby."

She says, "That's good, so then there will be two of you!" Well I should've shut up, but you ain't posta lie, so I just shook my head up and down.

Then she looks at her papers and says, "Hey, wait a minute. Aren't you one of the Gordons? There's more than two of you!"

I say, "There's some more." So she tells me to say the rest.

I go, "There's too many." And all the kids holler, "Well tell us!"

So I go, "There's Jean and Yvonne."

She goes, "But don't you have Mary? I had a Mary last year."

I go, "Yes, there's Mary too."

She goes, "So, is that it?"

I go, "No."

She says, "Well, who else is there then?"

I go, "There's Junior."

She says, "Junior? Is that his real name?"

I go, "What do you mean?"

She says, "Well, what's your daddy's name?"

I go, "Elmer." And everybody laughs because of Elmer Fudd. So then I ain't gonna talk no more.

She hollers at them, "No one will laugh in this class at another student!" Then she asks me if that's all there is. I shake my head. She says, "Well, hurry it up and say."

I go, "There's Johnny and Bev."

She goes, "Johnny and Bev. How many is that?" But I don't know how many I already said.

So I go, "I don't even know."

Then they all laugh and say things like, "He don't even know how many he has!" But I do know how many I have! I just don't know how many I already said I have.

Missus Gaylord hollers at them all again and tells them they won't get any milk and cookies. She goes, "I'm sorry, Frankie. Do you have any more?"

I go, "Did I say Mary?"

She says, "Yes, you did."

I go, "Did I say Pearl?"

She goes, "Pearl, no."

Then I go, "And there's Gracey and Johnny."

She goes, "You did say Johnny but you didn't say Gracey." I could hear them all laugh, but they don't dare laugh too loud because of them cookies.

So she goes, "Well! That's a great big wonderful family!"

Then I go, "Don't forget Charlotte!"

Then Missus Gaylord goes, "Oh my goodness, Charlotte?"

And I go, "Yes, and Lori too. But she's just a baby." So now all the kids start making funny noises like they was trying not to laugh. Then I look up at Missus Gaylord, and she's got a funny look on her face like she don't believe me, or like she don't feel good.

She goes, "Frankie. Did you say there's a baby named Lori?"

I go, "Well, she's kinda like a baby but she runs around."

She goes, "But didn't you just say there's a baby in your mommy's tummy?"

I go, "He ain't even born yet."

Then she sits down and says, "Well, God bless your dear, dear mother!"

I go, "Missus Gaylord!" I was gonna tell her they was laughing at me again, but then she starts laughing and waving her hands.

She goes, "No! Please! Frankie, no! Please don't tell me if there's any more!"

But I like all them I have! And I don't like her laughing. I want to run up and punch her, but boys don't hit girls. So I say, "Teachers is posta be nice," but she was laughing too hard and so was everybody else. Later she gives me more cookies than everybody else, like to make me think she's really nice.

The cookies was good, but that don't make her laughing right.

Later when I'm running with all them kids to jump on the bus, she yanks me over and says, "So Frankie, where do you fall in the line-up of kids?"

"Huh?"

"The birth order?"

"What's that mean?"

"I mean what number are you in the family? Where do you fit in?"

"I dunno. Somewheres in the middle, I guess." And I see she's gonna break out laughing, so I run away before she makes me mad again.

Later when we was all in bed laughing and telling stories, I holler over to the girl's room at Jean. "I like you guys better than all them kids at school."

She says, "It takes time to get to know people."

I say, "I even like the one inside of Ma's tummy better than them!"

She says that's because I don't know them yet. But I don't

even know the one inside of Ma's tummy. Except if you put your head right there, he kicks. You can tell he ain't gonna want to sit around in school, neither. Especially when they make him tell how many he has.

CHAPTER 13

WHO'S WRONGER, ANYWAYS?

In first grade Missus Silvernail is round like Ma, but she ain't got no babies in her. One day, she spanked Jamie Peterson because he was eating all the paste. She took his pants right down in front of everybody, and you could see his peterbug and hind end—and so could all the girls! So she did something wrong, too.

This girl sitting next to me says she ain't ever seen a boy-thing before.

I say, "They's different than girls."

She says, "They sure is."

Missus Silvernail spanked him real hard like I ain't never been spanked—even when that fire started on the floor. Ma says she didn't spank me because the house almost burned down—she says she did it because Gracey could've been killed in the smoke. But she only choked a little.

I say to Ma, "Well, we did it at school!"

She says, "What did you do?"

I say, "We made this Indian fire and we put feathers on, and we was dancing around the fire like the Indians do when they make it rain."

She goes, "Well, did Missus Silvernail start a fire right on the floor like you did?"

I say, "No. It was in a can. And then we popped popcorn on top of it."

She says, "Is that what you was trying to do in the living room?"

I say, "Yes, but I couldn't find no can!"

She says, "But if you burn up papers on the floor, Frankie, the house will burn down, and then your father will kill you!"

I say, "Well, you spank harder than Missus Silvernail!"

She says, "Oh my God, Missus Silvernail had to spank you?"

I say, "No sir! She spanked Jamie Peterson."

She grabs my arm and whispers like it's a secret, "What did Jamie do?"

I say, "I bet it was a lot worse than what I did."

She says, "We'll see about that when your father gets home."

I go, "You ain't posta tell on me!"

She says, "I don't have to tell on you—the floor's still wet from where I threw down water—and there's a big burn mark on the floor!"

I say, "You tell him Indians did all that!"

She says, "I spanked you like that so he wouldn't get after you too much."

I say, "I ain't going to school no more!"

She says, "Just ask me before you start any more fires, and you won't be getting into trouble—and don't you dare touch my matches again!"

I say, "Well, Missus Silvernail says cigarettes is bad, so someone should spank you, too."

She goes, "Well, here we go again!"

When Daddy comes home, I'm sitting at the big table really quiet, so he says, "You been crying." I don't say nothing back, so he hollers, "What's wrong with Frankie!" All the kids is in the other room, waiting for him to blow up. So Ma says to me, "Are you gonna tell him, or am I?" But I just sit there, poking the butter. So Ma says to Daddy, "You better come in here and see why I had to spank him so hard." Then they go in by where the fire was and start talking about me. I figger Daddy's gonna come back and knock me off the chair, so I start shaking like that time he cut my hair. But then I hear him laugh!

He comes back in the room and says, "You really are a wild Indian!" But I start crying anyways. Bev says if it was Johnny, he'd a got the belt. That's because Johnny looks like Uncle Shorty and Daddy don't like Ma's family. But they say I look more like the Gordons, so that's why he don't ever spank me. And Daddy knows Ma likes Johnny a whole lot, so he gets her mad when he licks Johnny. But he don't ever punch me or slap me or even switch me like he does Johnny. Or he'll tell Junior he's a gaddam lazy no-good rotten bum, but he don't say nothing to me like that. Johnny says I hide my bad stuff better, and Junior says just wait until I get older. But I think Johnny's right. Because if you watch the ones who get in the most trouble and how they get caught, you can make sure you don't do the same thing—or you do it where no one can see you. That's why playing in the woods is better than playing in the house.

Ma says, "Now Frankie don't want to go to school."

Daddy says, "Maybe he'll burn that Klump-dump down!"

But starting fires ain't why I don't want to go back to school. It's because they make fun of you. I don't care if Johnny or Pearl or Mary or Gracey makes fun because I do it right back. And anyways, we don't do it to be mean like them kids at school. Well, we do it to be mean, but you like them first. I mean, you like them before you're mean to them. But at school they don't even know you, so how can they like you? So when they're mean to you, it's because they're just plain old mean.

And I don't like to go to school anyways because they make you just sit there like they do at church and tell you to be quiet. Like at home, there's always some big deal going on, like everybody runs around and gets in big fights, and they play real loud when Daddy ain't home. But Missus Silvernail makes you sit there and cut paper and paste it and pretend you're a little sissy. Like she makes you sing dumb songs or hang on hands with them girls.

The school kids all laughed at me because I didn't say right how many I have. But how many you have ain't easy to say if you have how many I have. But Missus Silvernail shouldn't be showing boy's peterbugs to girls, so she's wronger than me. Except—oh yeah—she puts her fire in a can. Like big deal.

CHAPTER 14

JUST A SWITCHING

Green apples is good with lots of salt, but it gives you the squirts, so when Johnny threw that stone to knock the apples down, I was glad he missed. But then the rock goes way up and starts to come down by Vern's little girl.

I go, "Uh-oh." But the stone comes down and gets her good right on the head! She screams and the blood flies and Vern and Daddy come running down to save her. We was down by where the Devil is, which is maybe why it happened.

Then everybody else runs down—I mean like Ma with towels and all the big kids. They wrap her up good, and we all start up the hill, with her screaming like when Daddy cuts a pig.

Daddy goes, "What, did she fall down?" So Johnny starts to cry and says he done it with a stone.

Daddy hollers, "You hit her with a stone!"

I budge in, "We was just getting apples!" But Daddy jumps the ditch and rips off a switch.

He goes, "You don't throw stones around little kids!"

Johnny screams, "I was gonna give her an apple!" He jumps up and down like he's already switched. Ma grabs Johnny and screams, "Now don't you do that Elmer!" Daddy says them apples is gaddam green. Junior makes a fist like he's gonna charge Daddy, but when Daddy jumps back over the ditch everybody backs up. Then he starts in switching.

Vern steps in and says, "God, Elmer! It ain't that bad!" But when he says that, Daddy switches Johnny harder. So Johnny heads up the road screaming, with Daddy switching and Vern and Ma yelling for him to stop.

I was running behind Daddy's legs, watching it all. Johnny's got these little red lines on his back because he ain't got no shirt on. Every time the switch comes around, Johnny dances in circles, then Daddy tells him to stop jumping and he switches him again.

Ma's crying, "You care more what your friends think than you do for your own son!"

He goes, "He's just like Shorty!"

Ma goes, "Shorty don't beat his kids!"

Daddy goes, "Oh that's just a switching!" I don't remember what happened next because they all go inside the house hollering and crying and jumping up and down.

That night I ask Mary, "Why does Johnny always do things that gets Daddy so mad?"

She goes, "You just watch what Johnny does so you know how to stay outta Daddy's way." So maybe that's why he don't spank me—because I do watch like that—instead of because I look more like the Gordons than Johnny does.

I go, "Johnny's braver than all of us."

She says, "You're just saying that because he got switched."

Junior says he was gonna run in and grab Johnny, but he got thinking that might make Daddy switch him more.

I tell Johnny, "The next time you do a bad thing, you just say, 'Frankie did it!'"

He goes, "Ah, a switching ain't so bad." He lays there on his belly because his back hurts too much, and Ma had to rub this salve all over him and sing to him.

I say to Junior, "Well, the next time it happens maybe we all should jump on Daddy!"

He goes, "You ain't never seen him in a bar fight—even Johnny Gray's afraid of him."

Bev says one time when Junior was little he got licked so bad he couldn't walk, so Ma tells Daddy if that ever happens again, you're outta here, mister tough guy. But I almost don't believe what Bev said about that switching because Junior looks like Daddy's family way more than I do, so why would Daddy ever switch on him so bad? Acourse, maybe what Bev said is true because Ma likes Junior the best, so if Daddy did switch him like Bev says he did, Ma sure woulda said something brave like that to Daddy, even if she is ascared of him.

Bev says way back then Ma put salve on Junior's cuts just like she did for Johnny after he got switched. Junior was crying in that way you call a whimper because he was hurt so bad and only little, and all the big girls who was also only little back then stood around him crying too. And that all seems true, because when Johnny got licked so bad and was hurt and crying, I seen some of the girls go off crying too. It seems like girls don't have to get themselves switched to cry like they did get switched, but boys need a good switching to make them cry. When I ask Junior about his switching, he just laughs and says how there must be a good reason little kids is so good at forgetting.

Way later, everybody falls asleep, except me. I lay there pretending we had this trial for Daddy, like we did that time for the missing pop beads. We make him sit in the middle chair and ask him, "Why do you do them bad things like get drunk and slap Ma, or switch Johnny, or tell Junior he's a dirty no-good rotten bum? Or why don't you ever be really nice to the girls? And why did you cut Frankie's hair like that?"

But even in my pretend, I can't make Daddy sit there—he gets up and tips over all the chairs and we all run down the road. Then we all get brave and come back up and put the chairs right, and I tell him, "You have to sit there because I'm the judge!"

Then he swings his arms like he's in a bar fight, and he screams them swear words at us. So we run away again! After a while, I get tired of trying to make Daddy sit in that chair. So finally I figgered out how I could get myself to sleep. I just say the same thing over and over again like I did to make my toothache go away.

"Just a switching," I say to myself. "Just a switching. Just a switching. It was just a switching."

CHAPTER 15

LAUGHING ALL OVER

The way I see it, there's two kinds of churches, normal and Holy Rollers. I've been to both kinds, so I know. This time I'll tell you about the normal. Normal church is like the one Jean made us kids go to on Sunday mornings. She tells Daddy, "We're all going to church and that's that!" So she washes us all up and off we go. But when you get there, it ain't any fun. Like we go to Sunday school first, and they make you sit there just like it's regular school. And they do cut-outs of Jesus and put them on this board and tell you how he was so good. And then they show you the Bible and give you presents if you remember what it says. But who can do that when you can't even hear the Sunday school teacher?

Missus Farnsworth is like 90 and has these big thick ankles and she shakes when she talks and her voice goes up and down but she can only whisper and her teeth is gone. Bev says she's gonna die pretty soon and then we'll all be sorry. So I say, "Well what if she dies in class?" And she says to just go fetch the preacher and don't touch her. But I wouldn't touch her anyways because her wrinkles run everywhere and she's all spots and nobby. Charlotte says we should all hug her a lot because she was alive in the civil war, so she's loved Jesus longer. But I tell her I ain't hugging Missus Farnsworth and she ain't hugging me!

After Sunday school, you go to church and that's worse than Missus Farnsworth. They make you sit up straight with your hind end back against the pew so your legs go straight out and that hurts. If you wiggle, they say in your ear "Now you just stop that, mister!"

The preacher talks way too long, and you can't see him because the people in front of you are way too big. But even if you could see him, he just stands there like a post and says things nobody understands. The only good thing is you can stand up when they sing, and they sing a lot, so you get to kick around some then.

You can skip church if you get up before the big kids and go hide. In the summer, I go down by that old car in the field where Junior smokes when Daddy ain't looking. The girls can't make him go to church because he'll fight them off, so Yvonne tries to scare him there. She says, "I know you don't want to go to hell." But Junior don't scare and tells her if God is good like she says he is, he ain't throwing nobody in hell just for skipping church. That seems right to me, so it makes me not be so afraid.

Hell is where you burn all day and your skin falls off but you don't die. It's just like when the Russians drop the bomb and your skin falls off because the hot ashes fall all over you. Except when the Russians drop the bomb, you do die. And then you go to hell where you don't die. But only if you've been bad. Like way badder than skipping church. Anyways, I don't skip church all the time because sometimes they catch me in my hiding place. Jean says I get caught because God wants me in church. But I think God should've showed me a better place to hide.

Well, after a long and boring time in Sunday school, Missus Farnsworth dies like Bev said. And the whole church goes to her funeral. They say I should go too because she was my teacher for so long. I just have to wash my face and comb my hair. Ma says I shouldn't go because it will give me nightmares. I say I'll go because I never seen someone dead before. But when we get there, she's in that box with a lid on. Yvonne says Missus Farnsworth was so nearly dead when she was alive, it ain't hard to picture what she looks like dead. We all laugh at that and Yvonne gets mad because you shouldn't laugh at funerals and she meant it nice.

They sing all them church songs and the preacher points at the box they put her in and tells everyone how good she was and how she was just like Jesus, dragging herself to church every Sunday for so many years just to teach the kids she loved. And now she's where she always wanted to be. And then her kids stand up and tell how she was the best mom ever and some was crying. But the preacher says we should be happy for her and not sorry, because of where she is.

But this all makes us feel really sad anyways, and on the way home nobody's talking much. Bev says, "Well, she was alive in three big wars." Charlotte says, "I didn't know she was a nurse." Jean says, "Only God knows who a person really is." Yvonne says, "It's easy to miss all that."

I think of her big ankles and spotty skin and nobby hands and how she got all that helping soldiers shot up in them three big wars. I tell them I should've hugged her, but not loud enough so they can hear. Someone says, "Hey, Frankie's crying!"

Jean says, "Just let him sleep, he's so tired. We can carry him in." But they start tickling me and say, "Oh no! He's way too big for that!" So they get me laughing all the way home, and that's good.

That night when we're all dropping off, Yvonne tells everyone how Missus Farnsworth is in heaven with Jesus where she's
young again and not sick. And she's over us, right now, praying
for us just like she always did. But when I close my eyes, I see her
laughing, not praying. Like just laughing all over! And her spots
and wrinkles is gone and she's got these big white teeth and she's
dancing like Elvis with skinny ankles, and it makes you want her
back in Sunday school teaching all the kids she loves.

When it's time in school for show and tell, I wave both
my hands over my head so Missus Lake lets me go first. I tell
them all about the funeral, only I don't say the box had a lid on
it so they all think I saw someone dead, which makes the story
better for the kids to hear. When I got done Missus Lake looks
at me like I'm the one that's dead.

She says, "You mean your mother let you go to a funeral?"

I say, "No. She told me not to go."

"Your mother said you couldn't go, but you went anyway."

"Yes because Jean and Yvonne said for me to wash up and
go." I can see she thinks I done something wrong by looking at
a dead body, so I tell her it was okay to see Missus Farnsworth
dead because she was walking around almost dead before she
died with all of them spots and wrinkles and knobs and fat
ankles and no teeth. Acourse, all the kids start laughing at that,
even though I meant it nice. Before I even get a chance to
tell them it's okay that Missus Farnsworth died because she's
dancing in heaven now with pretty skin, Missus Lake tells me
to sit down. When I go to my seat, Missus Lake says she'll have
to think of a better way to do show and tell.

But I like my show and tell, and so do all the kids because
at playground they come up to me and make me tell them what

SOMEWHERES IN THE MIDDLE

it's like to see someone dead. So I lay down on the ground and pretend I'm dead in a box with the lid open. Even though I didn't really see someone dead, I figger it's good for them to think I did so when someone dies on them they won't be so ascared. Patty Galutia gets ascared when she sees me lay down like I'm dead and says she don't even want to think about someone dead, but I say it's all right because they get to heaven by the time your family goes to sleep that night.

Later I got to thinking how Ma might get in trouble with the school nurse if Missus Lake tells her Ma let me go off like I did to look at a dead body. So when none of the other kids is around, I tell Missus Lake how the lid on the box was really closed. She looks at me a while then breaks out laughing. She says one thing she's learned from seeing all us Gordon kids go through her class is how we come at life in a different sort of way.

"You children break the mold."

I don't get what she means, but the way she says it so nice I know Ma ain't in no trouble with the school nurse, so I get gone.

For a long time after that, I play this game by myself that I'm dead and all these people come to look at me and say how I was so good. Like in the woods or in class, I just lay there or sit there and try to stop thinking and breathing, which of course no one can do for long because life just keeps on pushing you to think things and do things even when you try to make it stop. But one day life does pull away and you do stop, just like Missus Farnsworth did. And then all these people come to look at you and say nice things to send you off. I figger, what can be so bad about all that dancing and singing and laughing all over heaven? All that seems way better than mosta the stuff they make you do down here.

CHAPTER 16

HOLY ROLLERS

Holy Rollers ain't like normal church because it's a lot more fun. Like when the fire comes down, people run around and jump and shout out "Amen! Praise the Lord!" And that's when the preacher's preaching! And the music's a lot more bouncy, and when you get blessed you clap and stomp and spin. One lady falls straight back with her hands in the air and don't get hurt! Charlotte says that big old bun in her hair saved her from getting knocked out cold, but Bev says it was the spirit that catched her, or an angel.

Ma says don't tell Daddy what they do there because he hates Holy Rollers. She says his Mommy was a Holy Roller at church but was wicked mean at home. Like she made Daddy sit inside and not play on Sundays after he worked like hell all week on the farm. She says Daddy's daddy left her when he got old because all her churching got the best of her. Then Daddy hopped a train to California. So now he says any of that praying in my house and I'll cut your gaddam throats. Ma says, "Oh please, Elmer!" Because she knows he ain't really gonna do it.

One day I told Ma to tell Jean and Yvonne I'm not going to normal church no more because it's too tight for me. She says that's what happens to little boys when they go to funerals. After I beg her for a while, she says I can go to Holy Rollers with Bev and Charlotte if I don't get carried away like Daddy says or start to think I'm better. Well, I'm not better, except I don't drink or smoke or swear or sleep around like harlots or watch TV. But it's okay to sleep with your brothers because you have to. They said if I signed a paper saying I won't do all that, I could join if I believe in Jesus, too.

The way I see it, Jesus is the one who makes the fire come down because it only happens when you're praying and you say the same things over and over like "Jesus! Jesus! Jesus!" Or "FIRE! FIRE! FIRE!" That's when all the big people start crying and get so blessed they don't care what they do or who's looking. But mostly they just run around with their hands flying in the air.

If they go on too much, the preacher steps in and quiets it all down and says things like, "You break anything in this church and it's not of God!" He means to say you take it all too far and then it's the Devil made you do it, like what happens in a bar fight. So that's how the preacher keeps it all from getting too carried away like Daddy says.

The only thing I don't like about church is not watching the Lawn Ranger and Twilight Zone and Alfred Hitchcock no more. When they're on, I set up chairs and blankets in front of me so I can't see it. Johnny says well you can hear it so why don't that send you to hell? But the paper I signed said I wouldn't watch no evil thing, not I wouldn't hear no evil thing. Ma says them making me not watch TV is just a way of saying they think they're better. But I tell her it's really just a way of keeping us outta hell.

Junior laughs and rubs my head and says, "How long you gonna keep this up ol' Fuzzy Head?" But he don't know I been praying the fire would come down on him, too. Like I bet he's doing all them things I signed the paper not to do. When the fire comes down, it'll burn all that right outta him. Then he can sit behind the blankets with me and just listen. And when the fire comes down, I'll make sure he don't get carried away. In front of Daddy anyways!

This one time when we was alone at home, the fire came down when I didn't really mean to make it happen. Mary Lou and me and all the little kids was the only ones at home because Ma and Daddy was gone two days and Jean got mad and made the big kids walk to town with her to get the food out of the car and carry it back home. So when the little kids got bored at home, I made them all get together so's we could play and pretend we're at the Holy Roller church.

I lined the chairs all up so they could sit in them like they was pews. Then I preached about how the fire came down that time on this man at church and he runs out to the street with his head on fire and hollering out so everyone could understand him even if they was from like Russia or China. Then I made all the kids get on their knees like we do when it's time to pray at the Holy Roller church, and I told them to cry out to God just like they do. Like you holler "Oh God, help us!" or "Send down the fire, oh God!" or "Jesus Jesus Jesus!" or "Fire Fire Fire!"

Then I told them to get up and run around the church, which was really running around the dining room table, and I tell them to start waving their hands. So when they do all that, I see Mary Lou is really crying! And pretty soon so is Pearl! When Gracie starts in, I know I started something I couldn't stop, so I start crying too. Acourse that made Chuck and Lori cry because they didn't know what was going on. Well, none of us knew what we was crying about, but when the fire comes down on you like that, it's like you don't really have to know. And so you just let happen what's gonna happen anyway because it's outta your control.

Like this one time when the fire came down at church, I seen this guy jump two pews and it seemed to me like he was way too old to do something like that. And I see all kindsa people run or fall down backwards and don't get hurt. One time this guy breaks down crying because he says he was mean to his grandma all his life, and she's the one that raised him because his daddy was in jail. And people holler out lotsa stories like that. It seems like if one guy gets on fire like that, then it jumps to all the others and then you never know what might happen. That's why I say going to the Holy Roller church is so much fun.

But when the fire came down at home the way it did, I got ascared because I thought we was just pretending to be in church, but then it turned into the real thing. So when all the kids start crying I start crying too, and I don't know how to stop something that wasn't me that started it. Pretty soon, though, it's like the fire starts to burn down and things get back to normal. Then you feel kinda stupid because you was crying so loud in front of everyone. Just about then, we see the big kids coming up the road with all that food. Pearl points out the window and says, "Hey, see what all our praying did!"

When we run down the road to meet them and Jean hears about what happened to us when the fire came down, she says she guesses it's okay to cry like that but sometimes it's better to just get mad and take charge of things. Yvonne says it happened because we was hungry. Jean says no one's going hungry in this family again if she's got anything to do with it. Junior says if

God can make you cry and jump around like that, why don't he make people come home with the groceries like they're supposed to. Bev says it's not right for Junior to blame God for what people do. Johnny says God makes us hungry so he can see who's strong enough to tough it out. Charlotte says God only wants for all of us to forgive and forget.

Seems like everyone's got something they think or want to say about God, and maybe he's so big all of them is right, I don't know. I do know one thing, though. I ain't ever gonna call down the fire again unless I'm in church or it's some kinda emergency.

CHAPTER 17

tHE PoP BEAD tRIAL

When Jean puts both hands on her hips, you know she's really mad, and there's gonna be big trouble if someone don't straighten up. She hollers, "Look! Vernene came over with orange pop beads and she's gonna leave with orange pop beads!" She says Vernene's daddy and ma will get mad at us, and then Daddy'll get mad at us because him and Vern is friends.

Jean has us all in the living room, and she says we can't go out and play until the pop beads show up. She tells Vernene to stop crying and not to pop her gum so loud. Vernene pops her gum and says, "You ain't the boss of me!"

Everybody's telling who they think took them pop beads, but you can tell they're just guessing. We all just got done looking all over the house for them, just in case they was lost and not stoled. Then Charlotte and Bev says we can find out who took them if we have a real trial. Jean says she don't care how we do it, just so we get it done before Daddy and Vern get home. So we line up all the chairs and put one in the middle for the trial.

Bev says I should be the judge because I always think I know who's right and who's wrong every time there's a fight. So they sit me up on the back of the couch. Then they tell me to call someone to sit in the middle. So I call Vernene.

Charlotte asks her what her name is and if she gonna tell the whole truth and nothing but the truth so help her God on top of the Bible. She pops her gum and says she just wants her pop beads back.

Bev says, "When you come over this morning, how many pop beads did you have?" She says she had lots and everybody wanted to play with them. Bev asks her why she wouldn't let anybody play with them.

She says, "There's too many of you to share right." So Bev asks her if she ever shares with her own brothers and sisters.

She says, "No way, them pigs."

So Charlotte says, "Well, maybe if you was nicer people would treat you better."

She says, "Them pop beads ain't yours." So Junior tells Charlotte to ask her where she had them last. She says Jean made her put them on the table and chased her out because the little kids was all crying to play with them.

So Charlotte says, "Then the last time you saw them they was on the kitchen table?"

She says, "That Jean out there was posta watch them."

Jean hollers in from the kitchen, "Like that's the only thing I have to do—watch pop beads for a spoiled little girl who pops her gum all day in front of other little kids who don't have any."

Vernene hollers back, "Go buy your own!"

Junior says, "How do we know you didn't take them pop beads and hide them on us so our daddy has to buy you more? Then you get enough to wrap around your neck and hang down to your feet!"

She says, "You seen me crying when they was gone."

He says, "Yeah, but you was blowing bubbles at the same time."

She goes, "What's that posta mean?"

He says, "You figger it out, Sherlock."

She says, "You're just mad because I got a hoola hoop."

He goes, "Yeah, I just love to wiggle my hips like you."

She says, "I can make it twirl around my ankles."

He says, "That's just because you're a skinny pole."

So I say to Vernene, "You're so smart, who do you think took them?"

She says she thinks one of the little kids took them because they wanted them the most, and boys don't like pop beads, except queers. So we get Gracey up there and do the Bible thing, but she's too little, so we have to tell her when to say 'I do.'

Charlotte says, "Gracey, it's okay if you took the pop beads."

She starts to cry and says she didn't do it. So Charlotte holds her and says, "Do you know who was playing with them last?" She says she seen Pearl with them on. So Pearl comes to the chair, and they do the Bible thing with her.

I say to Pearl, "If you don't tell the truth now, God will get you."

Jean hollers in, "God's not gonna get anyone!"

I holler back, "You can't tell God what to do, and anyways, I'm the judge!"

She says, "Well, don't let it go to your head, your honor!"

Junior says to forget the Bible thing because whoever took them is gonna lie anyways. So we don't do that no more.

Charlotte says, "Pearl, how much did you like them pop beads?" She says she likes them a lot, but she likes blue ones better.

Charlotte says, "But you like them a whole, whole bunch, don't you?" She says she does. Then Charlotte asks her if she likes them so much she might want her own. She says she wants a hoola hoop lots more.

So I say, "If we get you a hoola hoop, will you tell us where the pop beads is?"

She says, "You don't have no money!"

I go, "I mean if we tell Daddy to buy you one, will you tell us where you put them?"

She goes, "You buy me the hoola hoop, and then I'll tell!"

Vernene goes, "I'll give you my hoola hoop if you tell me where you put them pop beads!"

So Pearl says she put them back on the table. Then she tells Vernene to give her the hoola hoop. Vernene says, "You don't get the hoola hoop until I get them pop beads!" Pearl says she don't know where they are now. That seemed true because she would tell us just to get that hoola hoop.

When Mary gets up there, she says she thinks Bev took them because Bev was mad at Vernene for not sharing. Mary says Bev told Vernene that she's got to share and share alike when she comes to our house. But Vernene keeps saying, "You ain't the boss of me!"

So Bev says to Mary, "Well, why shouldn't we think you took them?" Mary says it's because she likes jumping rope better than dumb old pop beads or hoola hoops, and everybody knows that's true.

When Bev gets up there, she says there ain't no way she would take anything from a friend. Charlotte goes, "But did you invite her over?"

Bev says, "No, she walked here by herself."

Charlotte goes, "Do you think she came over because she wanted to play with you or because she wanted to show off all them new things?"

Bev goes, "Well, she likes to play with me, too."

Charlotte goes, "Yeah, but do you really, really like her?"

Jean hollers in, "Now don't you guys hurt anybody's feelings!"

Yvonne goes, "Sometimes Charlotte gets mad when Bev and Vernene play together." So Junior says maybe Charlotte took them pop beads because she was mad at Bev and Vernene. Charlotte says she ain't jealous because she can play by herself or with somebody else. And that's true. Like before when she was pretending she was on the Mickey Mouse Club and she dressed up just like Annette. She climbs the apple tree and sings this song that Annette sings about some boy who likes her a lot and then they get married.

When it's Johnny's turn, he gets up there like a wise guy. He falls down on his knees and pretends he's crying and goes, "I did it! I took them pop beads! Please don't send me to jail!" So everybody laughs at that. But I get him real good.

I go, "Hey! Johnny plays with buttons and that's something like pop beads."

He goes, "I do not!" but everybody says he does play with buttons.

He goes, "Well, if Daddy didn't drink we could have new toys, too!" But Junior and Yvonne tell him to shut up because Vernene was right there listening.

He points at me and hollers, "Well, at least I don't play with clothespins!"

I come right back, "They're lots better than buttons!" Because Ma gets clothespins that are round on top and look like cowboys, and she gets them kind you pinch that look like Indians.

He goes, "You can't even race with clothespins!" That's because he lines all his buttons up like cars and makes them race on this pretend track. He goes under the blankets and you can hear him say things like, "Number thirty-two takes the lead!" and "Number forty-one goes into a spin on the corner!" Then he makes this big crashing noise.

So we fight like that until Yvonne says clothespins and buttons is both good to play with, so shut up. But clothespins is way better because you can make them stand up or clip them on a box for a fort, and when you crash them all together it's just like a big war.

Then Junior says, "How do we know one of the little kids didn't take them pop beads outside?" So Jean says we can all go out and look, and she'll give a big surprise to anyone who finds them. So that means the trial is over. I was gonna make Yvonne and Jean sit in the chair, but everybody knows they wouldn't take them because they read the Bible too much, and they go to church when Daddy says they can. But he just don't want them to ram all over them hills.

I go to the kitchen and tell Jean, "I didn't take them pop beads." She tells me to go outside so she can clean the house. She says maybe she'll find them like we find Daddy's hat. I tell her I think maybe Junior took them because he likes to pick on kids. She says he won't pick on Vern's kids or he'll get a switching like that time Johnny did when he hit one of Vern's other kids with a rock.

I say, "Well, we should've put him on trial."

She says, "No, because it was an accident."

But I meant we should've put Daddy on trial because he hurt Johnny more than Johnny hurt Vern's little girl.

Jean goes, "Now you get out, too!"

I don't remember what Daddy did about them pop beads

when Vern and him came home because I tricked Johnny to take me up in the woods to find this old Indian trail before Daddy came home and says Johnny took them. I bet Daddy got really mad and hollered at everyone about them pop beads. But that wasn't the right thing to do, neither, because—guess what—the next day the pop beads showed up behind the couch.

Bev goes, "Like they didn't just fall back in there by themselves!"

Charlotte goes, "Maybe we should have another trial!"

CHAPTER 18

AFRAID OF BATS!

Daddy says when he was only little he worked in the barn at night and bats would come in the barn and fly around thick as bugs. He says if one gets on you, you just knock it off and go right on working because there's so much to get done.

He says when his brothers and him was cutting hay, rattlesnakes jumped out and bit them in the boots. But they just cut them in half with their sickle and buried their heads in the ground so a dog don't step on it later, because that would kill them really fast.

I tell Pearl to ask him if that field they was cutting hay in was the same field they cut across to run to school. Because one time he said kids back then all walked to school with no shoes on. And another time he told us how he ran to school all the way and had to cut across the fields to get there on time.

So I say to Pearl, "Ask him if a snake ever jumped out at him when he was running to school." But she don't dare ask him because he only tells stories when he's had beer, and he don't like it when you ask him questions about when he was a kid. I want to know if he really was afraid of bats and snakes when he was a kid, and if his daddy thought he was a sissy if he was ascared of them. Because bats can kill you worse than rattlesnakes!

Like if you're a bat, you fly in kids' hair at night and get all tangled up and crawl down and bite their necks. Then the kids get really sick, and all this white spit comes outta their mouths, and their eyes get really big and their legs get stiff and they clomp around and try to bite other little kids! So who wouldn't be afraid of that?

Like one night, Ma and Daddy was out and we was all watching Fright Theater on TV and this big old bat flies in the house. You can tell he's sick because he keeps flying back and forth and dropping down and jerking back up.

Yvonne goes, "He's got rabies!"

So the whole pile of us goes running and screaming upstairs. Except we forgot and left the little kids down there crying. So Jean tells Junior to go down and get them.

He says, "You go, you're so brave!"

She goes, "You got shorter hair!"

He goes, "Well, put a towel on!"

So we all grab towels and clothes and sheets and wrap them around our heads. Then Johnny and Junior and Bev crawl down the stairs to get the little kids.

Gracey's crying and says, "I want a towel, too!" So Bev grabs something from the clothes basket and puts it on her head and they start back up.

But right then Charlotte hollers out, "The bat's upstairs!" So everyone up there starts screaming and running around and pushing to be the first one down. Then the ones coming down the stairs meet the ones coming up the stairs, and they all crash into a screaming pile of kids. When we crash at the bottom, we all run and dive on the chairs and couches, and we sit there laughing at each other, all wrapped up in them stupid clothes.

Yvonne says we all have to sleep downstairs or the bat will

bite us in the dark. So the big kids crawl on their bellies up the stairs to get some blankets. They're up their screaming like, "There he is!" and "Look out!" So we get even ascareder.

I say to Mary, "What if Junior comes back down and he's got spit dripping down his chin!" She says then we got to do the same thing to him that we do to the bat. But he comes down okay.

Well, just when we all get covered up, guess who comes trooping home? Ma and Daddy.

Daddy hollers, "What's everybody doing up!" So we tell him there's a rabie bat upstairs. But he don't believe us because he says you can't tell if they have rabies. So I start flapping my arms to show him how the bat was flying up and down and backwards. He says that's stupid because that's how bats fly inside and for me to take them underpants off of my head.

I say, "No, sir! He's got this white spit coming outta his mouth!" He yells and tells us all to get upstairs. But no one goes because a live rabie bat scares us more than Daddy mad. So he gets madder and grabs a broom and runs upstairs and pretty soon you hear this WAP! WAP! WAP!

Then he comes downstairs holding a dead bat and he hollers, "You're all afraid of bats!" So we all get up there really fast because having Daddy mad at you is way worse than a dead rabie bat.

When Ma is tucking us in, I say to her, "How come when they're sleeping, Daddy makes them all get up, but when they're up he makes them all go to bed?" She says to never mind because it's just the beer talking. When we're dropping off, I ask out loud why Daddy ain't afraid of bats. Someone says why don't I ask why they're so afraid of him.

I say back, "No, really! How come he ain't afraid of bats?"

Someone says, "Don't you mean who's meaner—like Daddy or the bat?"

I say, "No! That ain't what I mean."

They says, "Well, what then?" But it's hard to say what I mean. So I say how kids today have too much sissy in them, but kids back then was all brave.

Junior says, "Well, that's easy to fix."

I go, "How then?"

He says, "When you get big and have your own pile of kids, you tell them how a swarm of bats attacked your family and how you fought them all off with Daddy's underwear!"

I go, "Just shut up!"

He goes, "Really! Then your kids will say to each other, 'How could Daddy be so brave?'" At first I'm mad at him for saying that. But when I crawl outta bed to look at the stars, it seems like he's right. It ain't running barefoot across a field of rattlesnakes that makes you brave. But telling about it later does.

CHAPTER 19

KILLER PIG!

If you're a kid and you're alone, you got to watch it because lots of things can kill you. Like if you don't stay with the big kids, you might drown or a rock might fall on your head or something might eat you up. And because you're so small, they can gobble you right up and then Ma would go, "Hey, where's Frankie, anyways?" Then all the kids would look around, but nobody would find you because maybe the thing run off with you and took your clothes.

Then everybody would get real sad and Ma would cry. And the big kids would tell the little kids, "Now don't you go run off by yourself like Frankie did."

If you was a pig and you was big and fat and you had these big horns coming outta your mouth and you saw two little kids and you got loose, you would run them kids down and tear them up, because Ma says pigs like to eat little kids.

You can run around and holler, "Oh God, help me!" but if they're already coming after you, God don't jump in—because lots of people get killed like that and he don't help them. He just gives you good feet so you can run really fast like Mary.

Like that time all the kids was down at the creek and me and Mary wanted a peanut butter sammich. Charlotte says, "You can go up to the house by yourselves, but if some old creep drives by you in a car and says, 'Heh, heh, heh. I got candy,' you run away." Or she says if you see any spies like that time me and Bev followed them Russians through the woods, you don't go after them today. And Junior says if you see this dead body floating down the creek, don't try to fish him out because he'll snatch the body outta the water when it floats down by where they're swimming. So they make us promise we'll go straight up to the house and come right back down.

Well, it's a long, long ways from where the creek is to our house, but everything's okay until we get up there. We just turned off the road and come up the driveway by this ditch Daddy dug so he can bring water into the house. Mary and me was jumping over that ditch when we hear this noise like a great big bear. We look over and it ain't no bear, but it's Daddy's big pig—and he's out. And he's mad at us!

Pigs don't like kids because Daddy cuts their throats and they scream like crazy when all the big kids hold them down. When Daddy cuts his throat just right, they all jump back, and the pig gets up and walks around and starts tripping over things. Daddy stands there with his knife in case he has to cut his throat again. I stand right behind Daddy's legs, so the pig don't get me, and pretty soon it falls over and dies. Then you can poke it and it don't even move.

Well, all them other pigs watched their pig friends die, and the one that's loose is the last one left. And he's mad because we killed all his friends and he knows Daddy's gonna get him next—so he breaks out and comes after us.

Mary goes, "The pig's out!"

I go, "He's gonna eat us up!"

She goes, "Oh no he ain't!" and she jumps backwards over

the ditch and spins in the air like she does when she's jumping rope. Her feet's already running when she hits the ground, so she takes right off down the driveway. But not me. I look over at the pig and see he's gonna get me before I jump that ditch, so I start running around in circles hollering for God and Ma to save me. But the pig keeps right on coming!

When he gets really close, I know for sure God ain't gonna stop that pig. And he ain't gonna make Ma hear me, neither. Right then it pops into my head that God gave Mary fast legs to get away—and maybe he did me too! So just in time I jump that ditch and take off over the field.

Mary's still running the long way down the road, and I'd a beat her to Missus Benet's, but the grass is really high and I have to dive under all them fences. But I can hear the pig right behind me, so I keep charging on. When Mary hears me crashing through the grass, she thinks I'm the pig after her—and that's the real reason she beats me down to Missus Benet's.

We go crashing up her porch and start banging on the door, but nobody's home. But that's okay, because when we turn around the pig's gone.

I said, "He's afraid of Missus Benet!" Mary says no, he disappeared because pigs can get the Devil in them. That's when I tell her where the Devil lives and how he's afraid of Jean and everything else Bev made me cross my heart and hope to die for.

That night when we're all dropping off, I ask Yvonne, "Hey. Do pigs get rabies?"

Bev says, "It don't matter if they do or not, if they eat you."

I say, "Well, I'd rather have a rabie bat come after me than that mean old pig because having bats chase you is lots more fun." Junior says that's because me and Mary have the only pig in the world that can jump a ditch. So hardy-har-har-har.

CHAPTER 20

REMEMBERING YOUR REMEMBER

In third grade, I wrote this poem, but Missus Hollister says the lines is all wrong and I have to do a new one that makes more sense. I tell her it's about how we remember.

She says, "If you want to keep it, try moving these lines around, and take out that word, 'Ugh!'" I give her a different poem that she likes better, but the one I really like goes like this:

> Remember
> I remember you
> You remember me.
> In my remember, I was standing here
> But in your remember
> You move me over there.
> In my remember you ate a bug,
> But in your remember you just said ugh!

So that's about how kids see the same things different ways, and how we remember different. Like sometimes I don't remember things they say really happened and I was there. Or sometimes I remember it when I wasn't there. It's like they tell a story at night and then I remember their remember. Then later I tell it like I was there, because I think I was.

They say, "You wasn't even there!" But I can see the whole thing when they tell it, and that sort of makes me really there. Or sometimes kids move people around when they remember. That's what Pearl does.

Like that time the Easter Bunny didn't come and bring our candy like he was posta. Pearl says maybe he did come but he didn't leave nothing because we was so bad. But Johnny says he didn't have time to come because he had to take care of those really poor kids.

I say, "Well, we ain't got much food, so why ain't we poor?"

He says, "We got food—it's just in Daddy's car and they ain't home yet." He says them other kids is really poor because they ain't even got a house or a car or ain't never seen the Lawn Ranger because they ain't got a TV.

I say, "Well, we ain't got coal."

He says, "Yeah, but stupid, Junior is getting some with the sled and he already chopped wood." We was all standing around the stove keeping warm, and the little kids was crying because they couldn't find no Easter eggs or candy or Easter baskets.

Yvonne says, "You just wait—he's still gonna come hopping along!"

Then she says how sometimes things take longer than the Easter Bunny thinks because there's just so many kids in the world. And anyways, she says Daddy might just see him hopping down the road because he's out there looking for him right now. So maybe that's why they ain't home.

When Pearl gets bigger and don't believe in the Easter Bunny no more—because her teacher lied and told her he wasn't really real—I say to her, "You remember that time he didn't come?"

She says, "No."

I say, "Yes you do—we was all around the stove and you was crying."

She says, "I was not!"

I say, "Yes you was!"

She says, "Well, there ain't no Easter Bunny, so he didn't *didn't* come."

I say, "But you was crying because he didn't come."

She goes, "No, sir! I just thought he didn't come. But he really didn't *didn't* come."

I say, "You thought he didn't come because he really didn't come!"

She says, "He didn't come because he ain't real, so that's why he didn't *didn't* come."

So I say, "Well, why was you crying then?"

She says, "Because I thought he really didn't come, but he really didn't *didn't* come."

I say, "No! If he's *really* real, he really *didn't* come."

She says, "But he ain't *really* real, so he really didn't *didn't* come."

I say, "No sir! If you say 'He didn't *didn't* come,' that means he really did come!"

She says, "That's only if he's real."

So we keep talking like that until all the words sound really funny and then they sound funny, funny, funny, and we fall down laughing and roll all around and that makes you dizzy.

I say, "If he ain't really real, then Ma and Daddy didn't *didn't* catch him on the road and get all that candy from him." So we start in again until we get tired of the Easter Bunny and go to Santa because one of those times he didn't come, neither.

She says, "You was crying by the stove, too."

I say, "No I wasn't." Because her remember moved me.

She says, "You was right there drinking coffee and Yvonne told you not to drink it, and you was crying." But I wasn't crying with the coffee! I was crying back in there by where Chipper sleeps and that was way, way later.

I say, "Well, Johnny was telling me to pretend I was eating that chocolate cake the Easter Bunny didn't bring and then he says, 'Here! Have some of this pretend cocoa and toast, too!'" He was saying things about all this good stuff until Yvonne tells him to knock it off.

Sometimes you cry if you get punched. And sometimes you cry when they pick on you. And sometimes you cry when you sing a sad church song, like Ma. And sometimes you don't even know why you cry, so you just cry, especially if you're a girl.

But it's stupid to cry over cocoa and toast because that don't make it come. And it's stupider to cry over the Easter Bunny because that don't make him come, neither. You don't cry in front of anybody unless you get hurt, and you don't ever have to tell them what made you cry. So that's why I went back in there by where Chipper sleeps.

Yvonne leans back in there and whispers, "You forgot your coffee, Frankie." She says she put a little more sugar in for me. Then she says not to tell anybody she done that or the little kids will want some, and coffee makes little kids stop growing. So that's why I know I wasn't crying when we was standing by the stove.

When Ma and Daddy come home, there's candy everywhere and they tell us they saw the Easter Bunny by the road. And all the kids is so happy and they're jumping up and down. And

there's noise like there is on hotdog night. But I didn't call no
one to the pitcher window because I wasn't watching for no
one. I'm standing there by the stove when Ma comes in. She
looks over at me, and I look right at her but don't smile. And
then she goes upstairs.

So I wait a little, but then I start to feel bad and go up
there, too. The girls are all around Ma, and she's sitting on the
bed, and she's crying and she says to them, "We should've come
home on Easter."

The girls tell her, "That's okay, Ma! We did alright!"

She says, "I seen the way Frankie looked at me."

I come jumping in the room and holler, "Hey Ma!" But she
don't even look up.

So I go, "Hey Ma! It's okay because you was looking for the
Easter Bunny!"

She says, "He was a long, long way away."

So I break in and give her a big hug and say, "You don't
even drive."

She says to the girls, "I couldn't get your father to bring
me home."

I say, "I like them Tootsie Rolls the best!" Then the girls tell
me to go down, but I was going to anyways.

Now if you ask them girls who got Ma to stop crying, they
think they did, because that's how they remember. But I know
that ain't true, because it was me. That's what I mean when I say
everybody remembers the same thing different ways. So I go
downstairs and start digging into that candy. Daddy is singing
songs and making the big kids talk to him.

I pile some candy in my shirt and go under the table so he
won't grab me to talk. Pretty soon Pearl comes under there and

says, "How can the Easter Bunny carry all that stuff?"

I tell her, "It's Easter magic."

She says, "Well, how do you know if he's really real?"

I say, "If he ain't really real then how did Ma and Daddy find him on the road?"

She goes, "Oh yeah."

Daddy's up there saying how he knocked some guy down and how them spicks run to the other side of the street when they see him coming with his brothers. And he tells how his daddy walks right up to a big old bull that got loose, and he hits him so hard he falls down to his knees and then the bull follows his daddy right back into the pen. So that remember was how the bull was afraid of his daddy, but everybody else was afraid of the bull.

Bev goes, "Wow."

And Charlotte goes, "Wow." And they was kicking each other under the table by my candy. I hear Junior whisper up there, "Well, that's one way to remember it anyways."

Mary goes to Daddy, "Well, why didn't the bull bite your daddy right back?" And that makes Daddy laugh.

And Charlotte and Bev start laughing too, but Daddy thinks they're laughing at him, so that makes him mad at them, so they run outta there. But I see his legs get up and follow them, and he starts hollering about his daddy wasn't afraid of no jews or mackeral snappers. So Jean makes him sit down and Junior brings his beer to him.

So that's how you remember in a house with a lot of kids. You try to remember what happened, but when they tell it the way they remember it later, you get it all mixed up. But that ain't so bad, really, and maybe it's good. Because if you was the only kid, you ain't got nobody else to remember what you forget. And then all your remembering goes somewheres out there, like a long, long way away, and just sort of never comes back.

CHAPTER 21

ANGELS ALL AROUND

When you've got twelve kids and Santa don't come like he's posta, it makes everyone really sad, except the big kids because they have to go around pretending to the little kids that they're happy he didn't come. They tell them it's because he's got a special surprise when he does come and that makes the little ones start to wait for Santa to come all over again, because it could be anytime. Like he might come down the chimney tomorrow or the next day or the next day after that. Well, we got a stove, not a chimney. But he knows how to come down that, too.

When we write our letters to Santa, we throw them in the stove and run outside to see the smoke come out the chimney and the little bits of burned paper fly away, because he reads smoke and paper like the Indians do—only he lives at the north pole and not in teepees. Sometimes Santa meets Ma and Daddy on the road when they come home and gives them toys to give to us to play with and lots of food to eat like turkey and coke and patata chips and patatas. And bread for toast, and butter and jelly. Ma tells the girls to make us all a nice meal, because she ain't up to it.

Well this one time, it was Christmas and Santa didn't come, and Ma and Daddy was away, so the little kids was sad all day even when the big kids tried to make them be happy. I watched out the pitcher window to see Ma and Daddy come up the road, but after a long time of them not coming, I fell asleep in the chair. But when they woke me up, everything was different!

It's almost dark and Yvonne calls us all together and says the big kids figgered out why Santa didn't come. She says he wanted to teach us that it ain't toys that make you happy but all of us all being together and having fun and playing nice. Then she takes us to the back window that looks way up the hill where you can see this big round moon, so even if it's dark out you can see enough to get around because the snow and moon makes the whole world like this great big lamp with yellow light.

When we look out, we see Junior way up there waving his arms by this big old pile of wood. He lights a match and up the fire goes! And that makes all the little kids be happy and scream because Yvonne says we are gonna do what people used to do when they didn't have cars or stores or stupid plastic toys to play with. So all the big kids jump in and get the little ones dressed for outside, but I can get dressed myself because I'm big. And they say how the snow is deep and good for slay riding down the hill, and when we walk back up we can get warm again by the fire and drink hot cocoa. And then you can slide down again, but you can only do it if you scream really, really loud!

So when the bunch of us get up the hill, we see Junior putting on more wood so the fire is burning real hot, and the big girls is singing all them church songs for Christmas. I look up through the fire and see them singing, and it's like they're angels coming down all pretty because the sky is black behind them, and the stars is blinking all around their heads, and the fire and smoke turns their faces into ghost-people that's really nice.

They try to get Junior to sing too, but he says his job is to get them slaying. So he gets all the kids that ain't singing together and says how we got to make this track going down the hill. He says after a few times going down, it'll be as hard as ice to slay on. We only got one short tabogin and two sleds, so we got to pile on top of each other all flat and our faces down, with the big ones on the bottom and the smallest ones on top. When the girls singing see what we was doing, they piled on too so they could help the little ones hang on and not get hurt.

The tabogin goes down first to make a track and then sleds go right behind. The first two tries is really slow like Junior said, but after that we start to pick up speed! Junior says when we get to the bottom, we got to make a sharp right turn which will throw everybody off, but it's better than crashing into that row of trees. And so off we go!

And that's why I say it's the best Christmas ever! Because when we pile on top of each other and take off down the hill and everybody starts to laugh and scream and hold on tight, I say to myself right then how this is way better than playing with stupid plastic toys. And I think how Santa's probably laughing when he reads the smoke from the bonfire because he knows we're having so much fun! And when you get to the bottom and go flying off the sled and crashing and rolling across that snow and you stand up laughing with all the other kids, it means you got no more worry in you about Christmas and all that other stuff. That's because playing like this is way better than what you was gonna do for Christmas, like get cap guns and cowboy hats and dolls and other junky stuff to fight over.

The only hard part is the big kids got to pull the little kids back up the hill on the sleds, so they get really tired after like ten times flying down that hill and crashing and rolling. So then they come up and sit by the fire and drink the cocoa that Jean made and scoops outta this big pan that's nice and hot. The little kids have to drink outta the big kids' cups so they don't spill and burn. Then we all sit on logs that Junior drug over from the woods and tell the stories of how we crashed across the field or seen other people crash and go flying.

After they was done singing Christmas songs, Junior says how Charlotte's gonna tell us all a story. She looks surprised and says, "Oh really!" And he says "Yeah. Oh really." He tells her to make it a Christmas story for the kids, the kind he seen her drawing on the stones. So Charlotte says she'll tell one if we all get in it too, and pretty soon we're all pretending to be them people and angels that's in the Bible. Like Chuck is baby Jesus, and Johnny and Mary is his ma and daddy, and the big girls are the angels singing, and me and Pearl are shepherds and kings because we got to play two parts, and Gracey is a sheep, and Lori is too—until she wants to switch to baby Jesus which we let her so she won't cry—and Chuck don't really know what part he's playing anyways. Then Gracey wants to be a sheep so we let her jump over to that from being a king. The way Charlotte talks the story out makes you think you're really in it, because she says how Jesus's ma and daddy was really poor like ours and so was Jesus poor like all of us. And he had to be born in this place that's not something to look at like our old house that Daddy's fixing up.

And when the angels come to sing in the sky, which was really the big girls singing, they say how the baby is something special, and Charlotte says that everyone that touches him gets special, too. So she makes us all line up and touch or kiss the baby Jesus—which is really Chuck or Lori, I forget. And she says when we touch or kiss him, we all have magic powers too, so we can see angels flying all around and watching over. I pull on her coat and say really quiet so they don't laugh how I already seen the angels, and she says she knows that but now I can talk to them too, like just before I go to sleep.

After we sled and scream some more, Jean says it's time for all us little angels to get ourselves to bed. And so we head on down the hill with the big kids carrying the little ones that's too tired to walk or asleep already. Johnny says how he ain't never seen someone roll across a field so far as me when we took that turn. I say well I never seen nobody go flying through the air like you and Mary! It seems like we all feel good for Christmas and nobody wants to ruin it by saying something dumb or stupid.

I look back up the hill one more time to see the fire burning down, and I see Junior standing there poking at it with a stick. I was gonna call for him to come on down, but then I see these angels all around him. They was in the fire, and the moonlight and the stars was blinking right on through them, but they was there alright, and I knew to shut my mouth. So I run right past the bunch of kids and on into the house.

When I was in bed and dropping off, I ask one of them angels what they was doing all around Junior by the fire, and she says they was blessing him because he worked so hard all day to give us Christmas. When I start to tell her that Jean and Yvonne and Charlotte and Bev worked hard too, she laughs and says how not to bring back all the worry that was slay-rided outta me. She touches my head and lifts me up floating, and when I look down there's the bunch of us sitting around the fire with the angels in it singing.

When Junior comes to bed way later, I hear him flop down hard and all the air puffs right outta him. I want to tell him about the angels and how they said he worked so hard, but it seems like words take magic all away. So I just lay there thinking and listening to him breathe.

"Junior," I say. "What we did tonight I never done before."

He's sleeping already but I hear him say back, "It's a big old world, Fuzzy Head."

"It sure is," I say to myself. "It's just a great big old world with Santa and angels all around."

Before I went to sleep again, I was pretending that Ma and Daddy was coming up the road and their car was full of toys that Santa gave to them to give to us. It made me think why Santa would give us toys like he does if toys was really dumb like Yvonne says, and if it's lots better to play together and be nice like we did tonight, without all that plastic stuff to be fighting over.

Then I got to thinking about cap guns and holsters and windup cars and dolls with eyes that pop open for girls, and I wondered if Santa remembered that I wrote him for a coonskin cap and not a dumb old cowboy hat. Like Davy Crockett's way better than Roy Rogers or Lash Larue. But Johnny likes Wild Bill way better because he carries two guns, so that's why Johnny's always after mine.

One time I asked Jean to hide my gun so Johnny couldn't take it. She says she can't be in charge of everything, but that ain't true because she is when Daddy ain't home. Like when it's hot out and we're all playing down at the creek, she even tells you where to go if you eat too many apples and what to do with it. Like she'll say go way over there by that tree where nobody can see and take a flat rock to cover it when you're done. But don't just drop the rock or you'll be sorry.

Sometimes angels make people play nice. Like they tell me I got to share my toys, or they make Johnny forget he wants them. But I like it better when people tell you what to do and make you mind and share your stuff. Because they say things that angels don't say or care about—like it's time to change that shirt or wash them jeans or your face has dirt all over it. And then they help you do it so it's done right. Angels don't do none of that.

After a long time of thinking like that, I get too tired to stay awake and someone hollers Ma and Daddy's coming up the road! But I'm back on the sled and screaming and laughing down the hill with kids all piled on top of me. They shake and shake me to get up, but I'm rolling soft and slow over the snow and farther out than anyone ever goes, and that's way, way, way more fun.

CHAPTER 22

WHAT'S REALLY REAL

When I got to be in the fourth grade and it was almost Christmas, Missus McIntyre hooks her finger like she does and wiggles it at me like I'm posta come up to her desk. That makes all the bratty kids laugh and giggle at me some more because they think I'm in trouble after telling them all what for. When they laugh, I want to holler how they're the stupidest kids on earth, but I know that would get me in the kind of trouble they thought I was in but wasn't. So I go up to her desk thinking how much fun it would be to tip over all them desks they was sitting in.

First she says loud so everyone can hear her how I ain't in any trouble, and she gives them her real mean look so they all shut right up. Then she leans down to me and whispers, "But you sure do have your troubles!" She says she's never seen a boy like me stand up to the whole class like I did at cookie time. At first I think she's saying that it was good I fought them off the way I did, but then she says most any other boy might think of changing his mind when he sees the whole class thinks a different way than he does about something.

I say, "What do you mean?"

She says, "Santa Claus. I heard you fighting with your classmates about Santa Claus."

I say, "Yeah! They was all saying how he ain't really real."

It all started when Patty pushes me and says how only little kids believe in Santa and how could a fat old man fit into a chimney anyways? Then Jamie Peterson laughs and says how could a kid so old as me believe that reindeer can fly? I tell them it's because they're jerks they don't believe in that! So Jenny Stout hears me holler that and comes running over and screams in my face, "Santa's like the Wizard of Oz!"

I say, "Who's that?" Which makes them all laugh really loud, so all the other kids come running over and get around me in a circle.

"He don't know who's the Wizard of Oz!"

I say, "Wizards ain't real!"

Some smart aleck says, "That's right! Just ask Dorothy!"

I say, "Who's Dorothy?" And that makes them all laugh together like they're one big fat mouth and belly. That makes me mad, so I tell them they're all getting coal for Christmas. That makes them mad, so they all start hollering at me all at once!

"He thinks deer can fly!"

"No I don't! Only reindeer!"

"Yeah, in cartoons!"

"Santa ain't no cartoon!"

And so we was fighting like that and getting louder until Missus McIntyre steps in the middle and hollers for us all to take our cookies and milk and sit right down and be quiet. Pretty soon she's wiggling her finger at me like I said and telling me how most boys wouldn't fight off the whole class like that.

"But not Frankie Gordon! Oh no! He gets all red in the face standing up for Santa Claus!"

Ma told me once there's always people in this world that

want to spoil Christmas for kids by not wanting them to believe in Santa, so I tell Missus McIntyre that. She shushes at me and tells me not to talk so loud. Then she puts her head in her hands. I can hear her breathe in and out like Junior does when he's gone off to sleep. All of a sudden she lets go of her head and puts both her hands on my shoulders.

She says, "You're a good boy Frankie. And I don't want to tell you what to believe, okay? But just promise me one thing right now."

I go, "Okay, Missus McIntyre. I promise!"

She says, "You've got to promise me you'll talk to your mother. Tonight."

I go, "I promise Missus McIntyre."

She says, "I mean about what's really real. Tell her Missus McIntyre wants her to tell you the truth about Santa."

When I promise her I'll do that, she lets me go sit down. On the way back to my seat, I'm gonna stick my tongue out at all them brats, but now I'm feeling dizzy and sort of carsick.

When the bus stops at the bottom of the hill, I'm the first one jumping off because I want to get to Ma before the bunch of them. So I run up to the house as fast as I can. When I get there, Ma's in the kitchen doing supper. So I tell her about the fight and what Missus McIntyre told me to tell her. All of a sudden Ma starts walking really fast around the kitchen and banging pots and pans. I can tell by how she's acting that there's something way off about Santa that she don't want to tell me.

She don't say nothing for a while, so I beg on her to tell me if he's really real.

"Well Frankie, I suppose it's time you know Santa's a myth."

I go, "He's a myth. What's that mean? Is he real or not?"

She goes, "Well, I just said he's a myth."

I go, "Yeah but is he really real?"

She goes, "Well, what's a myth, Frankie?"

I go, "You're the one that's posta tell me!"

Then she says it's a made-up story.

I go, "You mean that's what Santa is?"

She says, "Yes. He's a made-up story so kids can have more fun at Christmas."

I think about that for a while then say, "So he's a lie."

She goes, "No! He just ain't true for big kids. But he is true for little kids."

Right then I start to feel like I do when Junior spins me around, so I go upstairs to think it all out. Ma hollers up after me to not go and spoil it for the little kids who still believe. She says now I can be part of keeping the big secret. She was still talking when the bunch of them come busting through the door.

I'm up on my bed thinking about all the ways Ma and Daddy and the big kids all tricked me about Santa, and I'm feeling really stupid. But I'm really sad too that he wasn't really real, and I'm mad about how all of them brats was right and I was wrong. That's when Junior comes in the room.

"Daddy says to tell you to get your ass downstairs and eat something or he'll come up here after you."

I jump off the bed and hit him really hard right in the stomach. He laughs and says what's that for? I hit him again and holler how he made all them school kids laugh at me!

He asks me if they was laughing at my hair, so I go to hit him again but he grabs my hand and uses it to spin me in a circle. Then he picks me up and plops me on the bed.

"Why are you so mad at me ol' Fuzzy Head?"

"My head ain't fuzzy! It just goes straight up!"

"No really, Frankie. Tell me what's up. You know I'll beat the shit outta anybody who picks on you." He sits down next to me on the bed.

So I tell him about my fight at school with all them jerks and what Missus McIntyre said and what Ma said about Santa and how he's a myth.

He says, "God, Frankie. I know we was tricking all you kids, but I thought you knew what's real and was just playing along for the little kids. Like did you really believe Santa Claus is real? And you was fighting all the school kids about it?" I nod yes, and he flops himself back on the bed and slaps his forehead and says, "Oh shit."

I go, "What do you mean?"

He says, "You got one job, and that's to not make us all look stupid!"

I go, "Well you got nice hair and like five girlfriends and all them muscles and you can pitch baseball!"

He says it seems like I should've figgered out that Santa wasn't really real when he didn't come for Christmas last year, or the year before that. And I tell him that made him seem more real because Ma and Daddy didn't come home for Christmas neither, and they're real. So he tells me to get my ass downstairs like Daddy says and eat something while he figgers out what to do.

When I get to the top of the stairs, I hear him whisper, "By the way Sherlock, when I call you Fuzzy Head it ain't because of your hair." So he's like Ma when she says one thing you can take two ways. But you have to know what both things mean, or you can't figger it out what they're really saying. I was gonna holler all that at him, but then he would think I was even stupider and wouldn't help me with Santa and the school fight. And I was smart not to get him mad because he did figger out what to do.

The next day I go to school with a note from Ma that Junior wrote that says how Frankie got spanked for lying to all the kids that he believed in Santa Claus when he really didn't believe in him. So now he has to say he's sorry to the class or he'll get spanked again when he comes home tonight. Junior traced on the note how Ma signs her name so it looked real, but he tells me to be ready to say Ma broke her good hand if Missus McIntyre says it ain't her writing. But she don't say that. She just looks at the note, scrunches up her eyes and holds it sideways.

She says, "Your mother wrote this?"

When I nod yes, she smiles like she's gonna laugh out loud then gets ahold of herself and tells me to go sit down and she'll take it from here. Then she stands up in front of the class and gives this big talk about how we all know how smart Frankie Gordon is and how he is so smart he fooled us all into thinking he really believed in Santa, when he really didn't. And she tells them how I got in trouble for doing that at home and now he's sorry for tricking us all and from now on he says he'll use his brain to spell good and write good and do good math instead of making up silly stories about believing in Santa. Then she tells them all not to be mad at me for fooling them, or she'll write to Santa and they'll all get coal for Christmas. That makes all the kids laugh and scream at her because there ain't no Santa, and I scream right along with them, too.

Later I got to feeling bad because we lied to Missus McIntyre, so I went up to her desk and tried to tell her how Junior really wrote the letter from Ma. But she held up her hand to stop me talking.

She says, "Your sister was a valatorian and your brother is a genius! And you can tell him I said so." Then she gives the letter he wrote back to me and says, "And you can tell him I said genius or not, his handwriting still needs much improvement."

I take the note and tell her after what she said about me to all the kids they're gonna think I'm really smart when I ain't. She says to me there's different kinds of smart, and I have the best kind there is because I can see things real clear that ain't really there and that's called imagination. I ask her how she can know what I see, and she says she's taught tons of little boys and none of them can daydream half as much as me.

She pushes at my nose like it's a button and says real soft, "I see your eyes dancing all over back there when you're posta be doing math!"

Later when I'm out walking through the woods on the shortcut to the creek, I get to thinking about all the things most people can't see but really are there, like angels and Jesus and God up there blowing them clouds around and playing with the birds like he does. And I think how there's all these ideas that pop into your head that don't seem real at first, but then they do get real when you do the things you think about— like getting in an apple fight or building a snow fort. And then there's things that happened a long time ago that come right back to life when you remember them, like when Johnny ran into that big hornet's nest. And I think how you can close your eyes and see monsters and Russians crawling through the woods and hear bombs blow up and watch people's skin fall off and hear them scream because the hot ashes is eating them up and how it makes them stink.

All that got me to thinking how if you can believe all that stuff that you can't see, then maybe I wasn't stupid like they said I was for believing in Santa, because you never could see him neither. And even if he really wasn't real, it always made me happy to think about him flying all around and coming down the chimney with lots of toys. And even when he didn't show up on Christmas like he was posta, it was good to think he ran outta time flying all around helping them other kids who was poorer than us, and I could see them kids jumping around when they got up and found their cowboy hats and guns and dolls.

So guess what? I'll keep on telling the little kids Santa's really real even if he ain't. And when I get big and have lots of my own kids, I'll tell all them he's real too. Because even if he ain't really real like they say, in a way he really is.

CHAPTER 23

BAR FIGHt

One time I saw a guy get lambasted right through a plate glass window at the bar. Daddy didn't do it, but the guy that married Vern's daughter did. It all started when we was bouncing along this dirt road in the old green truck. All of a sudden Ma hollers out, "God, Elmer, we forgot the wedding!" Daddy slams on the brakes and spins the truck around so me and Pearl and Johnny almost go flying off the back! Then he hollers to Ma that maybe we can still make the wedding party. Ma tells Daddy to be careful of the kids, and he says they know they're supposed to sit down and hang on.

So we barrel on down to the Holcum's Saloon—Daddy calls it the Long Branch—and sure enough, just when we pull up, we see them two that got married walking through the door of the saloon. Ma says to Daddy how Betty—that's Vern's wife—is gonna be pissed. Ma never says them bad words, so I know she's really nervous.

We go in the bar behind them and Ma makes us kids go sit in the corner and says she'll send over some cokes—which never come, by the way, because of what happens. It's loud and smoky in that place like I never seen! Well, it gets smoky like that at our house too, but we just open the windows and flag it out with towels. Acourse, any flies that might be hanging around go right on out with the smoke too. And this place is louder than our house even when all the kids get fighting and playing at the same time.

It ain't too long before I hear this one guy say something mean about Vern's daughter in her wedding dress and how her hair is orange—like puffy and flying all around like she's on fire and really hot—like he was making fun of her. This ticks off her new husband who's hobbling around on crutches because a bulldozer knocked him in a ditch two days before the wedding. He stands there on one foot and puts his two crutches under one arm so's he can lean on both of them together, and then he takes his other arm and brings his fist way back like he's gonna let the wise guy have it. So I point for Johnny and Pearl to look and say, "This here's gonna be good!"

They call that punch a roundhouse in the old movies on TV—like the Mighty McGurk'll knock down two or three bad guys with just one big punch. Junior says Daddy would make mincemeat outta guys like the Mighty McGurk and he seen him do it. He says he hit this one guy so hard all his teeth go flying right outta his head! When they got sobered up, Daddy tried to buy him new teeth, but the guy laughed and said, "God no, Elmer, they was rotten anyways, so you done me a favor."

So anyways, when that roundhouse catches old mister wise guy, he goes flying back and trips over a stool and cracks right through that great big window! He ends up laid out flat on the sidewalk with glass all around him like he got hit by truck. Inside, all the men get worked up and hollering and shoving, so you know this is gonna get better. All the ladies go running off to the side, and Ma hollers for us kids to slide under the table. But we don't do that or how you gonna see the fight?

And it's getting really good until Daddy steps in the middle and spoils it all. I thought he was gonna start swinging like the Mighty McGurk, but he just stands there and rolls up his sleeves and talks strict like Mister Klump does when the teacher sends you to him for a talkin-to or the paddle. Daddy says anyone who takes a swing is gonna have to fight him because Vern paid for this wedding party and no one's gonna ruin it for his friend. The men get quiet and back off and one of them says, "Gaddam it, Elmer's right!" And then one of them takes off his hat to pass around for money so Vern don't have to pay for the window.

The bride's crying out stuff like how her wedding's all ruined until someone gives her a beer and makes her bawling stop. Then they all go outside to fix up the guy that got laid out flat and tell him how he deserved what he got. He sits up and rubs his jaw and looks around like he just got outta bed. Pretty soon he laughs and says, "Yeah, I guess I did at that!" When he stands up, he hollers out how he'll buy a round of drinks for everyone. Acourse that don't mean coke, so me and Pearl and Johnny don't get a drink.

Pretty soon the guy who got knocked through the window and the guy who knocked him are standing at the bar bumping each other's butt and laughing like they was best friends! Ma pokes Betty and says, "Ain't it just wonderful, the power of beer?" Acourse, the bartender was mad, but he got over it because they collected enough money to buy him a new window and give the place a coat of paint.

When Johnny Gray shows up, he's got his gun on, but he don't have to use it because they hid the guy who got punched because his face was black and blue. They all say how the window thing was just an accident. Ma says later Johnny Gray really knows it was a bar fight, but he ain't gonna tick nobody off and arrest them because it's a big wedding and all those people might not vote for him.

I was a little mad that Daddy stopped the bar fight and didn't show them guys what for, and I know he coulda done it. Junior says if he'd been drinking likker and not beer it woulda been a different story. But I seen enough to say how everybody's afraid of Daddy and Daddy ain't afraid of nobody and how he could take out the Mighty McGurk, even if he ain't real.

And I see how what Daddy did was good enough so Vern and Betty ain't mad because we missed their kids getting married. It helped that Ma told Betty we was late because Mary had to go to the hospital with a bad appendics. Lucky Mary, because now she'll have to miss some school or Vern's kids'll see she wasn't really sick and tell Betty that Ma was lying. When she goes back to school, Mary will have to hobble around for a while like she just had surgery, so maybe that will make the teachers feel sorry for her and give her better grades.

Ma said later the most dangerous place to be in America is in a bar on a Friday night. Acourse, we was there on Saturday morning, but it means the same thing. I tell her there ain't too many kids get to see a bar fight in real life like that, and she says don't go flagging that all over school.

Later me and Johnny set up a fake bar with lots of stuff on it so when he pretends to punch me I fall back and knock stuff everywhere. And that was lots of fun! Then he goes off and pumps his muscles up so he can be big like Daddy. Junior says if you're gonna be like Daddy, Johnny, you hit them hard and you hit them fast.

That night when they was all dropping off, I was thinking

about that bar fight and how it was almost like the Mighty McGurk, except when he wasn't fighting he was helping all the Bowery boys. And then he takes one home and says he's just like his own son. But all the church people who don't fight in bars and drink say the Mighty McGurk ain't good enough to take in a boy like that because he's such a barfly and a slugger. So when they was gonna take the boy away, McGurk says all this mushy stuff to him, and he turns away so the boy don't see him cry.

As I was dropping off, I was dreaming how Daddy's Mc-Gurk and McGurk is Daddy and Daddy picks me up and puts me on the bar and rubs my head and tells all them bad guys how I'm his son and how he's my daddy and how he'll fight for me if any of you swaggers go after him, and when they do he pulls that roundhouse out, and down they go and round they go, and out they go right through that big old window!

When I wake up it's too dark to go look outside, so I poke Junior awake and ask him which is more real to him, the Mighty McGurk or Daddy, and he says, "They both is stupid. But one gets paid for it."

He's breathing awake in the dark, then after a while he says to me, "Hey Fuzzy Head, when we go by the Long Branch on the bus, don't look out the window for Daddy's car or the bus kids'll know he's still in there drinking from the party, and that's none of their business." So I crossed my heart hope to die I won't look out the bus window for Daddy's car. Then he tells me I'm the best ol' Fuzzy Head there is and drops off to sleep again.

But I laid there awake thinking to myself how Daddy's got lots of McGurk in him but not so much as to ever make him cry or chase after no little kid.

CHAPTER 24

HoW tHINGS WORK OUt

I run way up the mountain, way above them trees I usta hide in when Jean and Yvonne try to make me go to church. I go way, way above our house where Daddy tells us not to go or the wolves will eat us. "Too bad, you mean old bully," I say to myself, "I'm going up there and I ain't ever coming back down, and you can't make me!" I run up through the bushes, breaking off branches and kicking everything that gets in my way.

When I get all the way up there, I look down at where we live. Our house is black—I mean like really black because Daddy ain't put no siding on yet, but we got a new roof. There's the pond the cow drinks out of when we have a cow. You can see the pig oinking around the pen. And there's that old falling-down barn below the house by where the Devil is. And way, way down from there is where Missus Benet lives.

The grass is tall and blowing where the farmers ain't cut the fields. It's autumn and you can see the hills all around. They look like that blanket Gramma made for Ma, all sewed up with them pretty colored squares. And there's the highway I usta watch for Ma and Daddy to come home on.

When I get up there, I walk a little slower. To make myself brave, I holler out, "It ain't really true about them wolves!" Then I come on this old dead woodchuck in the last field up. He's lying there in the grass. At first I think he's alive. But I step in closer and see his skin and hair's all falling off, and flies and maggots is crawling all around.

It's so ugly, I got to take a closer look. That's when I see these white bones sticking up outta him. With them flies crawling, them bones look like they're dancing in the sun.

Then I look up and see this pretty orange-yellow tree across the field. I run over to it and see how it's grabbing all the sun and pushing out a little breeze so it looks like it's alive, too. It's the prettiest thing I ever seen, so I go real close until the colors fill my eyes right up.

I go, "Seems like it's on fire!" And I stand there quiet—quiet like someone put a spell on me.

That's when I see there's a place under the lowest tree branch that lets you crawl inside. So I get flat and crawl down under that branch and go inside the tree. Then I wiggle myself up inside the branches and just sit there. Now the sun's coming through the branches, blinking at me. It feels good to be inside of something so darn pretty, so I sit there for a long, long time, just watching and breathing and breathing and watching.

Pretty soon it seems like some part of me is making the tree work because every time I breathe out, them leaves tickle and they rustle out this orange and yellow fire. But it's a good fire! The kind of thing that makes you think right, like when everybody's asleep and you crawl outta bed and go to the window to look at the sky. Or like staring into a campfire. I tell Junior watching them logs burn down helps you think right. He goes, "Just shut up, Fuzzy Head, and go to sleep."

Right then these two birds come in the tree. They're orange and yellow just like the tree and have some tiny, shiny black stripes. I know they see me when they come in, but they know I ain't gonna hurt them, and maybe they're even glad I'm there. They flutter all around, chirping and singing and jumping up and down on the branches. I sit there thinking, "Hey! They're trying to kiss!"

Then this chipmunk goes running through the leaves, so they scare off. But I think how glad I am that they came in. Right then it pops into my head that it don't really matter that we're poor as sin. Or that I have this stupid fuzzy head. Or that kids make fun because we have too many. Or that we live in this old black house. Or even that Daddy's sometimes mean to Ma.

Because I seen lots of trees before, but not like this. And I seen lots of birds before, but not like them birds. The kind of birds and trees that make you just stop. And that's what it is that makes you think right—when you just stop. Then you can see things better and you know what to do. And you know what's right. So the big kids don't have to tell you what to do no more.

Walking down the hill, I holler way out loud, "I know you gave her that black eye!" But she says she banged it on some door when they was out. But I see the big kids taking care of Ma. They put a washcloth on her face and was telling her to kick him out. She goes, "Oh now ... things just have a way of working out."

They say, "Well, he's done this before!"

She says, "Oh nonsense!" And that's when I took off running up the hill.

At first I was mad at Ma. Because running up the hill I wanted her to punch him hard, but I know she won't ever. Then I pretend I walk up to him and pick him up like I'm Superman and swing him around the room, and if he don't say he's sorry I throw him right through that big old pitcher window! Then I stand up there in all that broken glass, but it don't even cut me. And I put both hands on my hips and I look down at him laying there and he's bleeding and he's got this broken arm. I go, "I bet you're sorry now!"

But coming back down the hill, I think that maybe, in a way, Ma's right. You have a black house and old dead woodchucks and people making fun because there's twelve. But then them old dead bones come alive in the sun and these wow-like orange and yellow trees throw out fire. And things happen inside that tree that you hardly ever get to see, like birds kissing all in love. And I know then that getting blessed don't mean calling the fire down or running around the church and hollering "Jesus!"

And pretty things are there all the time, and they sing and dance and whirl around just like angels sing and dance and whirl around when they ain't mad and growling. So if you just look at black houses or people being mean or being dirt poor or little kids crying on hotdog night because their Ma and Daddy don't come home, you can get real mad and run away.

Coming down the hill, I say to myself, "If I go and get inside a tree every now and then, I won't ever have to do bad things like Daddy, or break nobody's arm."

Ma asks me where I was so long. I tell her I was way up on that mountain where Daddy tells us not to go. She says not to ever get myself lost up there.

I tell her, "I'm bigger now, Ma, so you don't have to be so much afraid."

She says, "Well, Frankie, what if you do get lost?"

I put my arms around her big belly and say, "That's okay,

145

tHE GREAt BIG SECREt

They put the little kids and me and Johnny and Mary outside to play all day. Ma was home and Daddy was at work and everybody was really quiet and nobody was fighting in there, so I knew something was wrong. Jean and Ma was upstairs all day, and the big girls and Junior was walking in circles and trying to listen up the stairs. When I peek in the window, Yvonne taps on it and hollers at me to have some respect!

Johnny says he seen Ma was sick, and Mary says well you get sick and have to lay down to have a baby, like the pigs. So we figured out Ma was having a baby and they was trying to surprise all the ones they put outside. But then why did Charlotte run up to Missus Gashay's to use the phone? And wasn't babies posta be born in hospitals?

We was out there fighting over where babies come out, when we see Daddy's car come flying up the road, and he don't ever drive fast! He goes even slower when he's drinking. Like he goes from side to side, but it's really slow so you don't get hurt. Sometimes he makes Johnny steer, like if the car goes in the ditch. Then Johnny thinks he's this great big deal because he gets to drive.

So anyways, Daddy comes tearing up our driveway and jumps out the car and hollers at us to play outside, which we was already doing. He leaves the door open a crack, so I figure I can walk right in because big people don't really see little people very much, like when they're talking or fighting or worried. Then you can watch and listen and figure out what's really going on. So I walk right in slow and careful and see right off they's all whispering about some big secret.

I find out what it is when I look on the table. There's this towel, and on it is this funny-looking thing. Daddy's telling Junior how not to name him, or we'll have to give him a real funeral and that's a whole lot of money. He says he don't know, but it might not be legal to just up and bury him, so we got to keep it really quiet so Johnny Gray don't come sniffing around. So I know right then I'm looking at a baby on the table, even though it don't really look like one.

Charlotte comes up and tells me he's a boy, but it's too hard for me to tell. She points to his little arms and legs. So I ask her why are they born that way, and she says well they're not unless they come out early and that means they're dead. I ask her if this is the one that was gonna come at Christmas, and she says yeah it was, but it's not no more.

So I sit down and start to feel really sad. I was figuring right along that when the baby was born on Christmas, Ma and Daddy would stay home, and it would be kind of like when Jesus was born on Christmas and everybody stands around holding each other and getting warm and looking down at the baby. And you know the good angels are all around even if you can't see them because they like to watch the little babies, too. Ma says when a tiny little baby smiles, it's because an angel's kissing him.

I see Junior close the towel around the little baby and put

him in this old metal lunch box of Daddy's. Junior looks down at me and says not to go blabbing and how I shouldn't be there anyways. I follow him out the door and see Daddy give him a shovel. Junior tells him he knows a good place, and then he crosses the road and cuts off through the woods. I know by the path he takes that he's gonna do the burying by the tree he climbs to see the world. All that's kind of scary to me. But it all seems kind of nice, too. I mean like taking care of a little baby that's dead.

Bev comes over to me and says how little souls live on and how the angels takes them to the clouds where they sleep until they grow up big like us. Then they go on and on and on, just playing and eating and singing with the angels, and they never get too hot or cold, and nobody smokes or drinks or hollers. She says there's lots of angels and babies up there right now, so he won't be alone.

I say, "Well how do they know what to call him when it's time to play?"

She thinks about that for a while, then says it's in the Bible somewhere they all get new names. I see that makes her sad, and she walks away.

I say, "Well how do they get a new name if they ain't even got an old one?" But she don't want to talk no more.

Junior don't come back for a long, long time, like when it's nearly dark. He goes in the back door and up the stairs like he don't want nobody to see him. So I go sneaking up there after him. He's lying on the bed, so I go over and poke his back. He don't move, so I try to shake him awake but that don't work neither.

"Junior," I say to him real quiet. "Junior, don't get Daddy mad!"

He sits up and turns to looks at me, and I see his eyes all red and puffy. He says, "What the hell?"

I run over to the window waving my arms and pointing out. I whisper so Daddy don't hear, "Junior! You left it in the woods! The shovel! You left it in the woods!"

He looks at me a while, then puts his hands over his face. He flops himself back on the bed and starts to do his chuckle thing.

"Good God, Fuzzy Head," he says. "To think there was almost another one of you!" He rolls up into a ball starts laughing and then gets laughing even louder. So I go downstairs hearing him laugh up there, thinking how maybe I did something good, even though I don't know what.

Charlotte always brings these flat rocks up from the creek so she can draw pretty faces on them. They got to be really smooth or the faces look all wrinkled. She lines them up for us all to see until the rain washes the faces all away, then she does it all over again. When none of them is looking, I sneak off with one of them really smooth rocks that ain't too big to carry and scoot it across the road and hide it by the telephone pole for the next day.

When the next day comes, Ma's still in bed and some of the kids is saying how she's gonna die because she's so white she ain't got blood. Ma hears them talking like that and hollers out for them to stop being silly, but we know Daddy didn't stay home from work for nothing. He sits there by the bed all day hollering at the girls to bring her things like wet towels and water and eggs.

Ma keeps waving him away and saying the baby's name, or what she was gonna name him anyways if Daddy let her, and Jean looks madder than I ever seen. Or maybe it's sad. So right then I ask Charlotte how to spell something, but I won't ever tell nobody what. It's a long word, but I'm really good at spelling from school so I lock it in my head by saying it over and over until I get done what I do next, which I ain't saying.

So I go outside and cross the road like I ain't posta and get my rock. I figure if they see me, I'll just drop it and say how I was on my way to get the shovel. What I do in the woods with that flat rock I ain't ever gonna say so Daddy don't get mad and Johnny Gray don't come sniffing around. It's a secret thing I do, but a good thing, too. And every now and then I go back there and do that thing again, like after it rains and what I do gets all washed off. So they ain't the only ones that's good at keeping secrets. And—oh yeah. When I come back, I forget to bring the shovel.

CHAPTER 26

WHAt BURNS YOU UP

When Ma don't want us so much in her hair or under her feet, she tells us to all go play in the creek until supper, but we can come back for a sammich if we get hungry, or we can pick berries on the mountain that's above the creek.

So off we go in a big bunch—not because she tells us to but just because it's so much fun! Heck, we even go there when she and Daddy is away. Only we can't go there until after Memorial Day or we'll catch polio from the creek.

So we all truck down there together if nobody's mad at somebody for saying something stupid. If they're fighting, they break off into these little packs of people that's getting along. It's a long, long way for the little kids to walk, so the big ones carry them, or if you ain't big enough to carry like me, you pull the little ones along.

We break off the road across this trail we made through the fields by walking it so much. You belly crawl under the barb wire fences that's here and there or you jump them if you're big. But you got to hold up the wire for the little kids and teach them to crawl under so they don't cut off their heads.

Junior's the one that makes it so much fun! He runs and splashes and pulls the scared ones into the deep so he can teach them to be strong because the water runs way too fast and wants to wash us all under and away. When the water gets running too low he says, "That's okay! We'll build a dam." He gets us all carrying rocks and sticks and broken tree limbs and pebbles and sand and big old clumps of grass and dirt to cram into the cracks, and pretty soon the water fills up and gets deep enough to splash and swim.

The creek bottom is really flat and smooth and long and steps down into the deep, so the big ones can swim there while the little ones play upstream, where the water falls soft over the rocks and makes these little pools for them to splash in. One time, I was halfway down and Junior comes splashing up to me and says, "I don't expect you to be so scared all your dam life!" Him saying that makes me jump off the ledge and into the deep because I know the water will wash me into him and he'll yank me up if I start to go under and away.

Sure enough! When I jump off, he grabs my arms and legs and throws me way up high like twenty times! I crash into the water and go under so much I know I'll never be afraid of Johnny dunking me again. Then he goes off and grabs onto someone else.

All that makes me really tired and hungry and mad that he went off to play with them. So I see to it the little ones is safe and playing nice and go up to lay on Turtle Rock. There's picture stories written all over it from when Charlotte and Bev was here last, but mostly the pictures is washed off. She drawed it with the colored chalk I took from Missus White's class so Charlotte could make her stories pretty.

When they catched me taking the chalk, I had to tell them what for and that made Missus White cry. So Mister Klump gets nervous and says I can keep them this time if I promise not to steal again, and he says he'll see to it that Charlotte gets lots of paper to draw pretty on. He says he'll have to tell my ma and daddy though. But before I could even start to cry and beg, Missus White starts to wave her hands behind me. I know that she's making signs because her waving makes my hair go crazy. She steps in and says to Mister Klump how that might not be such a good thing to do in this situation. Mister Klump looks at her blank, like he's dumb. Then he goes, "Oh, yeah. Elmer."

When I climb on Turtle Rock, Yvonne hollers up for me to not get burned, and that makes me think how if I did Ma would rub that salve all over me like she did to Johnny that time he got the switch. She rubbed and rubbed and sang quiet-like and wrapped him in a hot towel. And that was nice to watch.

So I lay on my belly in the sun and watch the creek wash over the stones, and the sun burns me into this hazy place where rocks and pebbles with the water washing over them looks like faces I seen and places I been or wished I been. And all the stories I been told come right to life, the true ones and all them lies, like where the Devil lives and Russians crawling through the woods and where Ma and Daddy go when they go away so long. And I see Junior throwing the ball until he gets tired and then he throws some more, saying how pain is good because it makes you be a man, but he's talking about the kind of pain that Daddy gives to him and Johnny and not the kind you feel when Ma's away.

And I see her getting in the car and looking back at me waving from the pitcher window, pretending like I really think she's coming home so she won't think I'm mad at her and make her feel bad. And the snow's falling on the slow deep tracks and the cars are making blurring haloes in the night. And there's me in the pitcher window dancing to make the little ones laugh and telling them how Ma and Daddy's gone a long, long ways away to get us toys because I know that will make them feel good, and they're so little they'll forget I even said it when Ma and Daddy don't come home.

When they all come running up to Turtle Rock, it's me they see lying there like burnt toast and feeling like the sun's dug a hole into my head. They drag me off and lay me in this little pool where the water is washing over the rocks and gushing onto me, and their words is swirling around my head. They're saying how I'll snap outta it pretty soon and how Missus Gashay will know what to do and how they got to get me home.

Pretty soon I'm sitting up and saying stupid things that make them laugh like how the Russians are dropping bombs and how I ain't a sissy and how I'm being washed away. They try to feed me berries to bring me back but I just spit them out, so they try to make me walk but my legs is wobbly and I fall down. So Junior wraps this wet towel over me and slings me over his shoulder. He jiggles me some and tells me to just hang loose and off we go! Some of the big girls is following.

Trudging up the hill, he says how Daddy'll knock him in a corner if he sees how I been burned.

I say, "He knocks you, I'll knock him!"

He laughs and says, "Yeah, you and what army?" Then he waits a minute and gives my bottom a whack.

I say, "Hey! What's that for?"

He says, "You're too dam sassy!" He jiggles me some more and says, "And get off the pity wagon. There's lots of kids got it worse than you."

I figure out how it don't hurt so much for him to carry me if

I do what he says and just hang loose, so I let my arms dangle.

After a long time of him carrying me over his back and the blood getting back into my head from where the sun burned it out, I say, "Junior?" He tells me not to talk.

I say, "Ma was crying because you're gonna join the navy."

He says, "That's not until after school."

I say, "Junior?"

He says, "Just shut up Fuzzy Head."

I say, "I don't want you to go, neither."

He was quiet for a while and I could tell from his breathing he was tired of carrying me. Then he says how that's the whole point of it. You grow up and go away. "We all do."

I think about that for a while and then I say, "Junior?"

He says, "Oh God!"

I say, "The towel's getting dry."

When we get up to the house, he plunks me on the couch and falls on the floor like he's been shot. The girls get butter and rub it where the sun made cracks in my skin. They feed me lots of water and bread and butter then put me on my belly so I can sleep before the pain starts in. They stick a towel under me in case I pee. Then I just drift off into that kind of sleep where you see good angels walking around and making the big kids be nice. And I see one of them hang over Junior and put a spell on him so he can't go in the navy and away.

And the last thing I see before I drop off is the bunch of us playing in the creek and the water washing over us like it wants to take us under and away. But we all hold tight, and it's all the bad things that gets washed away, and the bunch of us just hang there together pushing back at the creek all wet and laughing.

They hide me for the next few days so Daddy don't see how

bad I got burned and get mad at the big kids and hit on Junior. I smile when Daddy comes in the room so he don't see me hurting, but it's like he don't see me anyways. When we eat at the table I sit off to the side because when he eats he stares straight ahead. I always sit off like that anyways or at the little table in case Daddy gets all mad about something and starts to pound and holler or throw things.

I tell Johnny not to sit right in front of him, but he does anyways, which is why he gets in so much trouble. Like this one time Johnny wouldn't pass the salt and pepper to Bev, and so Daddy picks up this big butcher knife he uses to cut the pig and tells Johnny he'll cut his gaddam throat. Then he says how he'll throw him out the window if he don't stop all that sniffeling. Junior tells me he'd step in if Daddy ever tried any of that, but you got to know he don't really mean it. It's just Daddy's way of getting so many kids to mind.

After I get all better, Junior comes up to me and says how I ain't been acting right since I got burned and how he's afraid something happened to my brain in the hot sun. Then he rubs my head and says, "I know you, Fuzzy Head. You think too much. And I see you watching and studying everything and everybody. But life don't work that way." When I ask him what's he mean, he says, "I mean you got to get in there and live. Like live it up. It ain't all about playing it safe and figuring things out ahead of time so you don't get whacked. You got to stop hanging back so much. And live."

I say, "Well, how do you know I'm hanging back?" He says it's because he ain't ever seen me get licked. "Not even once."

I say, "Well Johnny's smoking, so he keeps on getting licked for getting caught."

He says, "Yeah, but at least he's out there jumping into it!" He tells me not to worry so much about getting licked because Daddy knows how to pull his punches and the main point of a licking is to scare you, not to hurt you. He says beer's okay but just steer clear when Daddy's drinking likker or coming off it.

I ask him if living it up is what we do at the creek, like when Bev jumps off Diving Rock and smashes her head on the rocks, or like when I jump off the ledge and crash right into him. He thinks for a bit and chuckles. "Yeah," he says. "That's it. Only then don't go and pull back so much like you do and start to think. Like you did on Turtle Rock. That's what burns you up."

CHAPTER 27

WHERE MA AND DADDY GO

Ma and Daddy stay home and don't go away for a long long time before they do go away and don't come back. Like they'll be home three weeks working on things like they're supposed to, then they take off. Bev says you can tell ahead of time when they ain't coming back after they go shopping by how Ma acts right before Daddy comes home on Friday, which is payday. She starts working faster in the kitchen, banging pots and pans too loud, and washing her face and looking in the mirror like forty times to make her hair just right. And she puts on a better dress, and she says no kids are going with them shopping this time out.

So me and Charlotte and Bev was wondering where they go when they do go away and don't come back, which like I said, ain't every week, just every now and then. Mosta the time they go away like three days and then come back. One time they was gone ten days, and after that I say to myself I'm gonna find out where they go if it's the last thing on earth, because they sure ain't ever gonna tell you.

So the next time Ma starts acting like she does right before Daddy comes home from work, I mean all nervous and such, Bev and I make a plan to jump in the car just before they go off to the store. So we do that, and when they come out, Ma says,

"You kids get out the car now." But we don't move, even when Daddy gets in and tells us to get lost. So when they see we ain't moving, Ma gives in like she always does when you really want to get your way. So when she says it's okay if we go, Daddy gives in too, and down the road we go.

Sure enough, they go shopping like they're posta and get lots of stuff to take back on the hill, but on the way home Ma says, "Hey, Elmer, why don't we stop at the Long Branch for a quick one."

Sitting in the car when they're in the bar tipping a few ain't no fun, and running up and down the sidewalk ain't either, especially when it's too dark to play because all you got is them blinking neon lights to see with. The bartender don't want kids in the bar on Friday nights because of all the fights, so every now and then me and Bev sneak in the back door and wave Ma over to us. If we say we're hungry, she brings us an orange soda or patata chips. You can tell when she's tipped a few too many by how her face is all red and her words don't quite line up when they come out.

So when it's getting dark, and it seems like me and Bev got to make a place to sleep in the car or maybe walk on home, up to the bar drives Chief and Andy Mess. They're these two guys that drives around in an old army jeep. They sure look and dress like bums, but Daddy says they ain't. He says they're real-life hermits, which means they go off to live by themselves unless they come to town for gas and beer. They've got the same last name because they're brothers.

Ma says don't ever ask them about the war or they'll freak out. She says they both was in it and got shot up pretty bad and they killed and mangled all sorts of Germans. She says they marched right into hell after Hitler, and just before they got to him he ups and shoots himself. She says they drink so much now so they don't have to think about what they did in the war, or if they hear a gunshot they won't notice it, or maybe they'll be too drunk to dive for cover.

She says she seen them dive like that in the Long Branch once when someone popped a cork. When they stand back up everybody's laughing so they laugh, too. Ma says she could tell they was a wreck, and so to bring them back to normal she hands them both a beer. Ma says Johnny Gray knows Chief packs a pistol and Andy keeps the jeep full of guns. Johnny just laughs and says if Hitler ever rises up again, they'll be ready.

So anyways, Chief and Andy go into the Long Branch, load up on beer and come out dragging Ma and Daddy. Daddy jumps in the car and says they're going for a little cookout and he'll drop me and Bev off home on the way. When Ma gets in she says me and Bev'll have to go with them or they'll lose off following Chief and Andy. She says they're squatting at a new quarry now and Daddy don't know how to get there.

So we go this pretty long ways following Chief and Andy who are driving all over the road right in front of us. Daddy laughs because of how Chief is driving, but me and Bev ain't laughing because Daddy's car is swerving, too. Ma tells him to let Bev drive but Bev she says she won't because she never drove a car. I know I can do it because I give the little kids ride on Daddy's tractor and wagon when he ain't home, so driving is easy for me. Acourse if I tell them I can drive, Daddy'll figure out it's me that's using up his gas, so I just keep it shut. It all turns out okay because we hit this back road which is full of ruts and rocks and it's getting too dark—along with all that beer—for them to see straight. So they have to drive real slow.

About halfway up this winding dirt road, Chief and Andy pull over to pee, so Daddy does that too. You can see Chief wobbling around in Daddy's headlights, pointing at his thing down there and hollering over to Daddy, "You got no choice when nature calls!" They're falling all over doing it, so Ma tells Bev to look away.

I turn my head away too, and when I do I see these two bright eyes shining down and blinking at me from the woods. They seem like nice eyes, so I get out slow and walk toward them. And pretty soon, right there, coming at me in the clearing, just as pretty as a sunset, is this crazy big deer with giant antlers reaching out in all directions. He turns sideways and steps so quiet through the brush you can hear his heartbeat. I lose him when he steps back in the woods and walks behind this big old tree, but then he bends around it and faces me directly. His eyes are big as saucers and when he snorts, even in the dark, his breath fills up the woods around him. He puts his nose to the ground like his antlers is too heavy, but then he rises up easy, just to show me he's in charge.

I stand there taking in the beauty of him until I hear Chief and Andy fumbling for their guns, and I know they see him, too. So I squat down, pick up a stick and scoot him off. When he steps away so large and graceful, I know I ain't never seen a thing so full of life and so sober. And when Chief and Andy go after him, tripping and crashing through the woods and shooting wild, I know I ain't never seen a thing so pitiful and drunk.

When them two brothers get back to the car and before I get in, Chief puts his hand on my shoulder and squeezes real hard, but in a way that Daddy can't see what he's doing. He bends down and with this yucky beer breath whispers in my ear, "I've been after that summa bitch for two years and I seen you chase him away. Let me tell you, if you wasn't Elmer's kid, I'd string you up in that deer's place and give you a dam good gutting. Gaddam sissy."

I look up into his eyes and see all his crazy from the beer and the ghosts of all the people he killed in the war and I know he would do what he said if Daddy wasn't there. So when he just shoves me off into the ditch, I'm kinda glad. When I told Ma later what he said, she says not to tell your father or he'll take Chief by his pigtail and throw him over the cliff.

I wish I could say the next three days was fun for me and Bev, but sitting around a campfire watching people drink all day and night is anything but. We had plenty of food from the groceries in the car, and Ma says for us to drink up the milk before it spoils, so if anything, the next three days we was overfull. There wasn't no lights or water in the house nearby. Ma says the people who usta live there must've walked away when the quarry shut down. Now what parts of the house they don't sleep in, Chief and Andy are chopping up for firewood.

On the second night, I get cold in the middle of the night and so I go over to the campfire which was kept going by Andy because all the others was nodding off. Ma says Andy don't ever sleep because of the war and thinking people and demons are out to get him. She says he's the nicest of the two brothers, but he follows Chief like a puppy dog because he keeps Andy in beer and food. She says both of them live off the government because they got medals for the wounds they picked up in the war and shell shock.

Andy looks across the fire at me and I can tell he's seeing

things that ain't really there, like I used to when I got really scared. Like this one time me and Johnny walked down to Missus Benet's to watch Superman on TV because ours got smashed for playing it too loud. On the way back home, it was dark and Johnny takes off running because he says that's the only way to beat out a bear. When he takes off like that it scares me so I just stand there hardly even breathing, and with things crawling up the road behind me you don't ever wanna see. I'd a been stuck there all night, except after a while Junior comes on down to get me.

When he's halfway down the hill, he calls out, "Hey there Fuzzy, come on up now. We're making popcorn!" His words feel like a rope to me and I use them to pull me up the hill.

"What'd you say," I holler back at him. "Did you say we're making popcorn?" Acourse I heard him right the first time, but I know if I can get him to holler out again I'll be safe until I make it to him. He knows I'm scared by the shaking in my voice, so he keeps walking toward me. Pretty soon he scoops me up, throws me over his shoulder, and even though we both know I'm too big for that carries me the rest of the way home. "God," he says, "if I was a monster, I'd eat you right up."

When I look at Andy across the fire and see the fear that's in his eyes, I know there ain't no words I can ever say that'll throw him a rope him or bring him back home, so I just stand there looking at him. His face is dark, all charcoal from tending the fire and old caked-on quarry dust that never goes away from never washing. He's mumbling stuff about President Kennedy and the Catholics taking over and the bomb that Russia's gonna drop and he goes on about flame-throwers and bodies squirming and people begging to die. But then, outta the blue he says, "You're the boy what chased away that deer." He pokes a stick into the fire and smiles nice at me. I see he's got no teeth. "When the sun gets up we'll take you boating."

I say to myself, "Yeah right! Ain't no way I'm getting on a boat with you two crazies." But sure enough, early the next morning Ma makes us all go, so we're all in this speedboat cruising through some winding swamp, with me sitting as far away from Chief as I can get. He's got it up to full throttle, gurgling down a beer and swerving to miss the stumps. He says later it's like this stump just jumps right out at him, so he corners a hard right which throws Ma backwards off the boat!

She under a long time, but then bobs up laughing. Bev's sure Ma's gonna drown so she throws herself in to save her, which acourse Chief, being so drunk, don't see. So when he pulls around, there's Bev's legs just waiting to get chopped up by the propeller. Long story short, Bev yanks outta the way in time, we all pull Ma back into the boat and everybody has a good laugh. So now it's Daddy's turn.

After a bit more crazy driving, we pull into a clearing which mighta been good for swimming except for them stumps and fallen-down branches everywhere and this mucky-looking green stuff all around the shore. Where the boat don't cut into it, the water's dark as sin. In the middle of it is this tall old tree, all dead with broken-off branches going up its side, which Daddy hollers to Chief above the motor looks just like a ladder. Ma tells him not to get any stupid ideas, but he makes Chief put-put over to it.

The timing was perfect for a guy so tanked and jumping into the air out of a moving boat. He grabs ahold of the first branch and up he goes, and I mean way up! Pretty soon he's looking down at us like we're little ants. Ma's screaming her head off for him to climb back down. Me and Bev can't do nothing but sit there and gawk.

He's way up there with his arms stretched out, swaying back and forth, which I figured could either be the beer in him or that old dead tree breaking under his weight. To make the dive work, he's gotta steer clear all them sharp and broken branches on the way down. He's also gotta gauge how deep the water is, which acourse he can't do because of the blackness of it. I ain't never seen Daddy play like his before, so even though Ma's screaming how he'll end up dead, I really want to see him make the jump.

I can tell he's got a plan in mind, and after a jerky hesitation and then a few fake starts, off the branch he goes and out—way out, I mean—and then down, down, down. His body's in the shape of a perfect dive, and it woulda been a perfect dive if his arms and head was pointing down. But he's laid flat out, aiming at the sun, and he never changes course, which lands him the biggest and loudest belly flopper that ever was. It's so loud and bad, Chief and Andy, who saw the whole thing coming down, dive for cover when his body cracks the water open.

He comes up laughing out loud how a thing like that'll sober you right up. Andy peeks over the edge of the boat and says, "Guess that'll fix ya fer having any more kids Elmer." Ma says later it was diving in his work clothes is what saved him from being split wide open.

Now you might think I'm telling this like all this partying is some great big fun. And maybe it would be fun if wasn't Ma and Daddy doing it and if it didn't go on so long you think it's never gonna end and all you can do is sit there and watch it play out because you're a kid. There's something about beer that makes people think they're having fun when they ain't really, or if they are, it's a kind of fun that I don't get. I mean, what's fun about not sleeping or eating or talking straight?

Later that night when we was sitting in the car and they was over by the campfire singing and smoking and drinking, I says to Bev, "So this is what they do when they go away?" She says, "This or something like it." I tell her we've been here two nights now and I wanna go home. She curls up her legs and rubs them where the propellers almost chopped them off. "It ain't about what you want or what I want," she says, "because it ain't about us. Is it."

"Bev?"

"Yeah?"

"When we get home you won't tell Johnny I ate all the patata chips."

She thinks about that for a while and says, "Not if you don't tell Mary I drank all the milk."

"Frankie?"

"Yeah?

"The next time I come up with a plan for us to go away with them, would you push me off a cliff?"

I sit there thinking about something smart to say back, but all I could do was chuckle, which acourse sets her to chuckling, too. And pretty soon we're laughing with the kind of laugh you do when something ain't really all that funny but there's a stupidness to it that's outta your control.

The next day Chief takes me off into the woods with a bag of empty beer bottles and his two favorite guns. He says, "When these here go off they'll kick the sissy right outta ya." I gotta admit it was fun to do all that shooting, even though shooting off a shotgun hurts like heck and makes my shoulder black and blue. And it was fun even if I only blew up every other can and even if I didn't like the guy I was shooting with. This one time I picked off three cans in row, so I says to him, "So who's the sissy now?" He looks at me, laughs and says, "I'd wager you're bout halfway there. To being a man, I mean."

This time when I look up into his eyes I see something different than I saw that first night when I chased the deer away and he was gonna gut me. In the dark that night, I saw the badness, but here in the light of day, I see that one of his eyes is glass, and his forehead's pressed in around it from where, I guess, some German clubbed him.

"You wanna be a man," he says, "look no further than your Daddy. He's the hardest dam worker I ever seen, and them that works with him say ain't no carpenter can hold a candle. Why me and Andy woulda died off a long time ago if it wasn't for Elmer showing us how to cut stones from these deserted quarries. And even if I only got one eye, I can see you judging him."

Way too loud I say, "I wanna be a carpenter like him when I grow up," but even as I say it, I'm mad at myself for trying to cover up my sins for someone I don't even hardly know or like. On the walk back he pulls a beer from his pocket and pops it open. He's a chugger, and when the beer kicks in, he starts to mumble.

"I know I'm a worthless piece a crap." A little further on, "Trust me, I wouldn't be here if it weren't fer taking care of Andy." And then, "That dam war it was that made him such a wreck." I know there's things that should be said to a man who's feeling so down and out. But they can't be said by a kid who's never seen nor done nothing, good or bad.

"Hey Chief," I say, "Next time I get a crack at him, I'll shoot that deer myself!"

He snaps out of it, stops and looks slow through the woods, then up at what sky you can see through the trees. His glass eye sparkles when it catches a bit of the sun. "Ah God," he says. "I miss my people."

When we finally get back home, Ma and Daddy drag around for like three days, Daddy with a limp from hitting the water so hard. But he makes himself go back to work and Ma takes charge of the cooking and cleaning again, or what charge you can take when you got twelve kids. You can tell all the kids is mad or jealous of me and Bev going away with Ma and Daddy for so long. Acourse it didn't help none that we only told them the good stuff like Ma getting throwed backwards off the boat and Daddy nearly getting killed from that high dive.

When you go to bed at night and it gets quiet after all the kids drop off, you can see things better. I tell myself I ain't ever going off with Ma and Daddy like that again. And I ain't ever gonna eat food that's meant for the other kids to eat. I thought a whole lot about that deer I seen in the woods. Just when it's my turn to drop off, he comes up slow and shows himself to me, so big and beautiful and sad. I tell him I was lying when I said I'd shoot him dead. He blinks, rises up, snorts and steps careful away, right outta my dream. Or, I don't know, maybe into it.

CHAPTER 28

SHOE-WALKING

In sixth grade, Missus King has me in the back of the room. She's sitting right next to me in the chair of a kid who's out sick. She's small enough to sit in it without squeezing herself outta shape. She's a nice lady, but she's real nosy, too. She's telling me how the world's a pretty friendly place if you let it be so, and how it helps a kid grow up if he'll learn to walk in other people's shoes. She says when you do that, you'll see that people in the world ain't all bad or scary.

When she tells me it's good to walk in other people's shoes, she just means to say how it's good to see what other people see and get the feelings they feel when bad things happen to them. Then you might like them more because you'll see they got problems just like you. She says you might think someone's walking around all mean and grouchy, but if you walk in their shoes for a mile, you might learn they're dying of cancer or maybe they got a kid that don't sleep or there's something else that's really terrible happening to them. So maybe they ain't mean and grouchy after all, but they're just plain ol' worried.

Missus King is saying all this because she says she wants me to step out and be more a part of things in class. She says I'm full of good stuff waiting to come out, and if I do let it out, then the other kids will like me and be my best friends. She says she knows I got all kinda smarts by how I do my homework good without even taking it home, but it's not my brains she's worried about. It's my attitude that gets to her. She says it's like I really ain't even here in class half the time.

She says President Kennedy got to be president because he asks himself what he can do for the country and not the other way around. She says he's trying to walk in all our shoes at the same time, and that's why everybody loves him so. Then she says she wants me to write a paper on how President Kennedy and his wife and kids got to live in the White House. When she says "the White House," I think of our old black house on the hill and then my mind goes drifting off up there and to all the bad stuff that's been happening. When she hears me sigh and sees my eyes roll back, she jumps up all mad.

"Hey lady," I'm thinking when she stomps off to her desk, "why don't you try walking in my shoes before you go dumping some stupid paper on me? Maybe I got things to worry about that you don't see." Like Ma and Daddy's been gone four days and Junior is mad at them because he and the other big kids got to take care of everything now that Jean and Yvonne are gone, and that's because when Jean came home from college Daddy kicked her out because he don't want her going off to school like she does, and then Yvonne got mad at Daddy for kicking out Jean and she went running down the road with her!

When I ask Ma why Daddy is acting so crazy even when he ain't drinking likker, she says it's because he loves us all too much, but he don't know how to show it except to scream and punch at what he don't like. I tell her I bet he don't do none of that at work. She says that's because the men at work do what he says and when he says it, even though he ain't the boss. But raising so many kids is like driving a bunch of cats down the road, and it drives him crazy that he can't keep us all together on the hill. That's because all us kids have a mind of our own, and he don't understand that's the way it's supposed to be, because his ma made a slave outta him. I ask her what his boss thinks about Daddy acting like he's the boss at work when he ain't. She says his boss laughs it off and tells everyone he can sit on his hands whenever Elmer's on the job.

I never did write that paper for Missus King, but what she said got me to thinking how hard it is to walk in other people's shoes. I mean, how can you see what other people see and feel what they feel when you have to spend all your time seeing and feeling your own things—like how are the little kids supposed to get ready for school all nice when the big kids get kicked out and Ma and Daddy go away? And you can't really do what Missus King says anyways. I know because I tried walking in the shoes of Bugsy.

She's this girl in class that comes to school with bugs in her hair, so that's why we call her Bugsy. On Valentine's Day, she was the only one that didn't get no cards when we passed them around to each other. She was crying in the back of the room until Missus King made her this great big red card in the shape of a heart that said she was the best valentine in the whole class. Acourse that made all the other kids jealous and hate her even more. Some of the rich kids said they was gonna rip up her card on the bus, but I don't know if they ever did.

Well, I tried to walk in her shoes one time, but I couldn't because she's a girl and wears a dress. And girls cry more than boys do and for different things, so I couldn't feel her feelings neither. And then when I think about her and all those bugs crawling through her hair, I start to itch. I saw I couldn't do none of that shoe-walking like Missus King says, but when she wasn't looking, I sat in the back of the class and just stared at her for a long, long time.

The next day I got to thinking maybe it's a good thing to try walking in someone else's shoes even if you can't do it, because after I watched her like I did, I didn't want to pick on her no more and I never called her Bugsy again. I got to thinking maybe her ma and daddy's too poor to buy kerosene to put on her hair to kill all them bugs, so it wasn't her fault she brings them to school. And maybe she wears that same dress every day because she ain't got no more to pick from, or the salvation army is outta her size.

When she sees I ain't picking on her no more, she starts to smile at me a lot, but I don't smile back or all the kids'll think she's my girlfriend, which she ain't ever gonna be. Sometimes at night though, I think about how cute she is when she smiles at me like she does, and I feel sad that no one's ever gonna tell her that somewhere under all them bugs and dirty clothes, she's just as nice and good as the rest of us. And why do rich kids pick on poor kids anyways, just because their ma and daddy give more and nicer things to them?

So then after that, I tried to walk a mile in Daddy's shoes, but I couldn't do that, neither. That's because it's hard to be around him when you know he might blow up. It's like he's got this stick of dynamite in him that's got a fuse that's always burning down, and you don't know when it might explode. I heard him say to Ma once how all us kids go outta the room when he comes in. He says to her, "You work it out so they like you better." Right then I knew he didn't even know about that stick of dynamite, or even that everybody's afraid of him.

Sometimes I'm upstairs and I don't come down when he's home, and not just because he might make me go pull weeds in the garden, neither. It's like he don't know what to do when he ain't on the job or working outside at home or downtown drinking. You can hear him walk from room to room downstairs. When I listen close, I can tell which room he's in, and I can even guess good how long he's gonna stay there before he walks into the next.

Bev says after he kicked Jean out and Yvonne ran down the road after her, she saw him looking out the back window and he was crying, but that I never did believe. That's because I ran upstairs when he blew up at Jean, and when I listened to him walking around downstairs later, the sound of his steps was mad, not sad. Anyways, there ain't no way you're ever gonna make a guy like Daddy cry.

You can't walk in his shoes even for a little ways because he don't talk to you unless he's tipped a few, and then it's the civil war or what life was like when he was little, when men were men and not a bunch of pussies. He tells how his brother Rex went to Texas to be a ranger and shot these guys dead that was stealing from the railroad, but he don't ever say nothing about what it was like when he was little, like was he ever scared, or why did he quit school when he's so good at math, or did he even like to be around his daddy? And what really made him hop that train to California?

Junior laughs and says Daddy's all about rocks, not feathers. I think he means Daddy can do hard things but not soft. That's why he can take a tractor all apart, wash it down with gas, and put it back together. Or he can knock down walls and then build up a new house, or he can dig holes and go to the quarry and bust up rocks with a sledgehammer, then hammer and chip them into nice long stones. But he can't ever hold you or say something nice like I'm glad you did so good in school, Jean—or your boyfriend's nice, Bev—or Junior, you don't have to have so many girlfriends and drive a hot car to be a man.

When I was real little, I never wanted him to come home from work except for them cupcakes in his lunch bucket which he never ate. I didn't know about that stick of dynamite way back then, but I could see this dark was over him that made him look at us kids like we was always wrong. When I got religion later, I saw there was these demons all around him like the kind was after Jesus, but I didn't know how to fight them off because they was even scarier than him, and anyways, he didn't even know they was there, crawling up his back. One time when he was drinking likker for a long time, I could see them demons looking straight at me through the red in his eyes. Ma says that's why they call it demon rum.

In a funny way, it's him liking to drink so much and spend all that time with his friends at the bar that makes things get better at the house, even if things don't get done like they should. That's because when he don't go to the bar for a long time, you can feel that fuse burning down and you know what's gonna happen. So when he does go off to the Long Branch, it feels like the house takes this great big breath. But then you feel bad you want him gone so much because he's your daddy and thinking that way makes you feel like a sissy because you're afraid of him.

When I get big, I'm gonna shake him up and holler in his face how this ain't no way to be a father when you kick out the big kids that takes care of the little kids just because you think everything has got to be like it was when you was young. And maybe it wasn't so great back then anyways because your ma was so mean you ran off to California. And you shouldn't be mad at us kids because you couldn't go off and fight Hitler because you had too many kids, because you're the one that made us!

I heard Bev and Charlotte talking about why he goes away so much and takes Ma with him. They was guessing all sorts of things, and I piped up and says how it ain't none of what they said. I tell them Ma and Daddy go away because there's too many of us. They say, "No Frankie, it ain't about you or us. It's about him." But I know if we wasn't all borned, he wouldn't take off so much and spend all that money he makes on his friends at the bar instead of buying siding to cover up the black of our house. But I could tell Charlotte and Bev didn't want me to say or think things like that, so I pretended they talked me out of it.

I grabbed ahold of a kid's hair the other day. He was crying and screaming something awful, but I wouldn't let go, even for the bus driver. We had all just piled on the bus and this kid was singing some stupid song about Bugsy, trying to make her cry. But that ain't why I pulled his hair. When I sat down behind him, he stops singing and whispers something to the boy sitting next to him. I figured he was talking about our old black house because he was pointing at something up our hill and laughing. Acourse, he didn't dare say nothing out loud or Johnny woulda nailed him.

So I grab ahold of him from behind and make him cry like a baby in front of everyone. All the kids was laughing and screaming, and the bus driver was hollering at me and trying to pull my hands outta that mean kid's hair. I only let go when Junior comes over and whispers in my ear, "The kid's a jerk alright, but guys don't pull hair, they punch." When the bus driver starts driving, Junior says something to the kid which makes him sit up straight and stop his crying. And whatever Junior says to him, he don't ever come after me or tell Mister Klump what I did to him. And—oh yeah—he don't ever pick on Bugsy again, neither.

Later Junior asks me if I kinda gotta thing for Bugsy. That's because he thinks I pulled that kid's hair to stop him from picking on her. I wanted to tell him why I really did it, but I didn't want him to get any madder at Daddy for drinking so much and not finishing up the house. So I tell him I ain't sweet on her, but I just don't like no rich kids picking on poor kids. He looks at me and laughs. Then he gets all serious and says, "Jeepers, Fuzzy Head. You ain't the Lone Ranger!"

After the fight on the bus, which wasn't really a fight because I was pulling hair and not punching, I got to thinking about Daddy and why he is the way he is. You can say it's because there's a dark cloud over him like I used to when I was little, or he's got demons crawling up his back, or there is a stick of dynamite in him waiting to blow. But all that's just ways of saying you don't really know him or why he does what he does.

So you make up these picture stories in your head which gives you a quick answer so you don't have to think or guess about it no more. Then when you look at those pictures you made up about him, you can tell yourself you got it all figured out, even though you only just made him into something he really ain't. Then you don't have to feel so bad when he comes in the room and you walk out, because demons and dynamite and dark clouds is smart to get away from.

When Ma heard what I did to that kid on the bus, she says, "What are all the bus kids going to think about you now?"

I knew right off that they'd do the same thing to me that I've been doing to Daddy. They'd say things like, "Hey, don't sit by that crazy Gordon kid," or "You never can tell when that boy might blow," or "There's some dark cloud or demons pushing him along."

And all that talk and the way they treat you like you like you ain't even a person is the kind of stuff that makes you want to hit on someone, or up and quit school, or maybe even hop a train to California.

CHAPTER 29

tHE KID WHO DOESN't CARE

When you got twelve kids in your family, there's gonna be fights in school when you get big because some wise guy's gonna say something about what your ma and daddy do to make so many of you and you're gonna smack on him until he takes it back. That's what Johnny does. So his whole class knows you keep your mouth shut around him or you'll get knuckled good, and sometimes more than that.

With me it's different though. I ain't got as much to work with as Johnny does. And I was doing okay about staying away from being picked on until a city school closed, and we got stuck with a bunch of them boys who was mad because they had to go to school out to the farm—that's what they called our school. And a lot of them was tough from learning how to wrestle and box at the Y.

The Y's too far for us country kids to go, and who wants to do that anyways when there's creeks and woods and fields to play in? Sure, they can punch real good, but they wouldn't dare to let a bull chase them across the field so they make it just in time to dive under the fence. And they probably think it's stupid to climb up and bend over trees like Junior used to, or line up a buncha kids on each side of the creek and have an apple fight. So they think we're stupid hicks, and they know we can't fight them off when they come on like gangbusters, two or three at a time like they do.

It ain't too long before these new kids hear I got twelve kids in my family, and then the fun begins. Three of them get me in the boys room saying nasty stuff about Daddy, which shoulda earned them all a bloody nose, and it sure would have if I was Johnny. I can see these bullies are trying to make me swing first so they could say I started it. Then they'd a punched me to the ground. At first I think of scaring them off by saying my brother's a boxer, but then I figure they'll go after him. So instead I tell them Mister Klump's my uncle, which they only half believe, but believe enough to let me go.

I know from watching Johnny grow up that I'll get muscles pretty soon, just not soon enough to take care of these here bullies. Thing is, I started school early because I'm so smart—or because Ma wanted me out, depending on who you ask—but either way, starting early makes me smaller than the bullies and mosta the other kids. I do everything I can to keep myself away from them, but they're everywhere! In class throwing spitballs and in the halls dumping your books and throwing punches and pinching as you walk down the hall. All that happens every day, even when they think Mister Klump's my uncle.

One kid comes up behind me before the teacher got to class and boxes my ears so hard my brain does a somersault. I scream out and spin around real fast, swinging wild. I bop him in the nose before I see I just hit the biggest bully of them all. The teacher walking in right then's the only thing that saves me from a good pouncing on the spot. I spend the next week dodging that no-good before and after every class and spying for him up and down the halls. I know he's out to get me, which

I'm sorry to say he finally does, in gym class.

They made us play football and acourse the coach thinks these new kids are the bomb because they go out for all the sports, and so he lets this bully kid keep squaring off with me when we go up to the line. I wish I could say I'm tough enough to hold my own, but before the class is over I get pushed back, smashed down, stomped on, walked over, head butted, and punched and pinched so many times I'm a just a bag of broken eggs by the end of the class.

"Gotta toughen up there, Gordon," is all Mister Ginther says when he sees me limping and dragging off the field.

I don't sleep much any night that week for worrying about what might happen the next day with all them bullies, so I think on it quite a bit. Johnny has a good way to deal with the loudmouths and bullies, but it's plain that won't work for me. He goes in fast and takes them by surprise with a good punch to the gut. Then he's all lined up to give'm a black eye if that's what they deserve. He says even if they come back and take you out, at least you got a good one in and it gives them something to think about before they run off their mouths again. I guess he knows how to take a few good knocks from Daddy licking him so much. So it's quick-in, quick-out for Johnny, but my bullies are too big and too fast for that.

So then I try to think of what Junior does to fight off bullies, but I come up blank. That's because I never heard of him fighting anyone in school. He is a baseball star and a girl chaser, and when he graduates he'll win the award for history. He's gonna join the navy to be an engineer and he don't ever get in fights, so I figure maybe there's something I can learn from him.

Acourse there's no way I'm telling Junior about the bullies who're beating on me, because he'll step in to help and that'll only make it worse for me when he's outta here. Besides, I don't really want him to know they're pushing me around and saying the mean things they are, or that I let them do it. So I think of a way to get his help without him knowing he's helping me. That's the sorta thing you learn to do when you grow up in a big family like mine and everybody's doing their own thing.

I go to Ma looking all sad and tell her I want to be more like Junior is in school but I don't know how. And then I say the same thing to Charlotte and Bev. Just to make sure it sticks, I go and say it to Mary, too. I know they'll run right to Junior because they're girls, and girls like to fix things that's broke, especially boys.

Sure enough, in a few days, here comes Junior! I can tell his head's all swelled because everyone's told him I want to be like him in school. He put his hands on my shoulders, walks me up the stairs, and steers me into the bedroom. He walks me across the room, spins me around, points to the bed and says, "Sit!"

He walks around in circles with his hands on his hips smiling at me with that crooked smile of his. At the same time he's smiling at me, he's looking me up and down. Pretty soon his forehead goes into a frown and he's looking at me like I'm all covered with warts.

"OK," he says. "I'm giving you one lesson. After that you're on your own."

He says right off, there's one rule and one rule only, and here it is: "You get the girls, the guys will follow."

"Huh? What's that mean?"

"It's simple," he says. "The more friends you have, the more you're gonna get. See?" I shake my head no.

"It's easy, Frankie. You start with the girls. That's the easy part. Then, when the guys see you got girls all over you, they want in. So they make like they're your best friends just to get near the girls. And pretty soon the guys are following you all over, just waiting to see what you might do next."

I really want him to tell me how to take care of them bullies, so I say, "Well, what if one of those guys gets jealous of you and starts to punch you or push you around?"

He looks at me like I'm on cloud forty-nine.

"Pay attention, Fuzzy Head. This is about the girls! You get the girls and everything else follows."

"That's easy for you because you're the pitcher on the baseball team and your hair stays down and you got muscles and you always know what to say." He sits down next to me and says "That's all true enough. But getting through school ain't about none of that, I swear. It's about what you do with what you got. And if you don't have anything, you just pretend you do. Jesus, Frankie, I learned all that early on."

He slaps me on the back and jumps up "This here's what I mean." He points both hands at himself. "When the girls look at me, what do they see?"

"I dunno. They see Junior, I guess."

"You say that because you don't get it! No, they don't see me—they see what I want them to see. Like when I'm being really cool, they see a little Elvis. Or when they see me acting all sad, there's just a touch of James Dean. And when I'm clowning around … I dunno … they see the Big Bopper!"

All that seems way off track for me, so I flop back on the bed. He gives my sneakers a kick.

"All I'm saying is get your head outta your butt and be whoever the heck you want to be!" He points his fingers at me and says, "Just don't be you, because that's nowhere, man. Dig it?" Sometimes Junior talks like a Maynard Krebs, but he ain't really a beatnik.

"Yeah, I guess so." But really, I just want him to leave.

"No. You don't get it. Here. I'll show you." He goes over to the closet and opens it up. "You can see I ain't got that many clothes here, right? But that don't mean crap because I do something a little different every day. Like one day I put my collar up." He puts his collar up. "And the next day I put it down, but I untuck my shirt." He does that. "The next day I might roll up my pant legs. Or maybe I don't wear a belt and keep my zipper halfway down. Or I roll my shirt sleeves up and stick my cigarettes in there."

He shows me how to do all that, like I'm too dumb for words. "And when the girls look to see what you're gonna do next, they don't even see the rest of you. All they see is the cool." He's so excited he throws his hands in the air. "It's like they don't care where you come from, only that you're here!"

He says pretty soon all the guys are doing what you do. One day he says he brought a yo-yo to school and by the end of the week the whole class had one. He says there's nothing half as cool as a hip guy swaggering down the hall with his shirt out and collar up, walkin-the-dog with a bright orange yo-yo.

I ask him how he can have so many girlfriends at one time, and he says he don't really have that many, because he don't latch onto any one girl or let any of them latch onto him. He says being cool is staying loose. He says people will think you're latching on, even if you ain't, because they only see what they want to see, not what's really there.

He says, "Look here, Frankie, the whole idea is to get through school in one piece and have a little fun along the way." I wanna say, "Yeah, like getting kicked from one end of the school to the other," but I don't.

So then he makes me do all that he just did, like walking with my collar up and my shirt untucked, and strutting around like Elvis. When I do all that for him, I can tell that I don't come even a little close to pulling off the look he's going for. He studies on me for a while and says, "Shit. It's your hair." So he goes to the dresser and picks up a tube of this goop he uses to make his hair slick back, like James Dean.

I can feel the grease when he rubs it in, but it ain't thick enough to make my hair stay down or go the way he wants it. It just keeps springing back up after he presses on it. Pretty soon he gives up on me, wipes the goop off his hands onto my shirt, and steps back outta the room. When he gets to the door he spins around and hollers back, "Just be cool, kid! Maybe it's the sort of thing you grow into." When he gets to the end of the hall, I hear him whisper, "In your case, that's a great big maybe."

At first I'm thinking Junior was no help to me at all, and I'm really mad at him. Or maybe a little jealous. But then I get to thinking some more about what all he said. Yeah, he didn't teach me how to take care of them bullies like I wanted him to. But he did teach me that people see what they want to see when they look at you, and if you pull off a few good tricks you can help them see what you want them to see. Acourse, first I had to know what I wanted them bullies to see. And to do that I had to know how they see me already. And to do that I had to know how they think.

It's hard to see how a bully thinks unless you know one pretty good. But you don't get to know bullies because they don't want you to be their friend, which is why they pick on you so much and try to show everybody how strong they are so everyone gets ascared of them and stays away. Sometimes it seems like they ain't too smart, like a caveman ain't too smart. But then sometimes it seems like they're way smart, because they know how to get what they want, and they always get what they want, just like Junior is smart and gets what he wants. The only difference is Junior acts like he does to get a lot of friends, and bullies do what they do to chase people away.

All that gets me to thinking about what a bully really wants and if it's true he really don't want friends. Maybe he thinks it's enough for people to look at him and say how tough he is or how much of a man he is, even though he ain't really. I mean just about any kid in the next class up could take out any one of the bullies that's pounding on me, so how can they really be all that tough? They're just pretending that they are. It's kinda like Junior pretending he's got all the girls, even though he don't really have any one girl that he's latched on to, but everybody thinks he does.

All that thinking makes me all bothered and don't help me know what to do to get what I want, which is to stop the bullies from picking and pounding on me. When they look at me, I want them to see a kid that ain't worth it to pick on, but I don't know how to do that. That gets me thinking about the kids that I pick on and why I do it to them and why I don't pick on other kids that I could pick on even though it would be easy.

Acourse, I don't ever pound on no one because I ain't big enough. When I pick on people, I just do things that drive them crazy, like hide their pens or put tacks in their chairs or say things that's true but not nice, like call them Dumbo if they got big ears or Pinokio if they got a big nose. I figure that's okay because they say mean things to me about being poor or how many kids we got in the family. None of that stuff makes kids like you, but they ain't gonna like you anyways.

Thinking about the kids that I don't pick on is how I figure out what to do. At first I couldn't even think of who they are I don't pick on because they're the ones you just walk right on by like they're ghosts walking down the halls. They're the do-nothings setting at their desks whose mamas bring cookies to the teacher's room so their kids'll get more help. Every now and then, these kids'll squeak out some answer the teacher wants to hear. Mosta the kids I don't pick on is girls, because boys don't pick on girls, except girls like Bugsy, which I usta pick on but don't no more. But a lot of the ones I don't pick on are boys, too.

These kids are kinda strange because you can't figure out where they come from or what they do after school. It's like you don't even see them until they come outta the mist and sit down at their desks. You can look at a bully and know what his daddy's like, or you can look at a guy like me and guess what's up with me and my family. But these here quiet ones are such that you don't even want to know. They're like that guy in the movies who plays the invisible man, except they never get into any kind of trouble like he does.

Right then I knew I had to figure out how to become invisible like them. The stuff I already don't do, like answering dumb questions in class, or taking homework home, or even the stuff I do do, like skipping school and cutting classes—all that stuff just makes you absent, but not invisible. Because when you come back, the bullies still pound on you. Being invisible means no one wants or even thinks to pound on you because it's like you ain't even there to see, like them good kids I never pick on.

Then it struck me that I already do what they do all the time, only I get invisible at home. Like when Daddy's on a drunk and hollering about the spicks and niggas and jews taking over, you just pretend he ain't there, which is the same as pretending you ain't there, which is being invisible. Sometimes he grabs and yanks on your arm and goes on and on about the civil war, but if you just hang loose and flop around a little, he forgets you're even there, which to him you ain't. Then he lets you loose and you go play.

This one time I didn't get invisible and he almost broke my arm. He's all on a drunk and crying about how his Uncle Bill got his arm shot off at the battle of Bull Run, and because we just talked about that in class, stupid me says, "Well if your Uncle Bill was fighting for the north and for Lincoln, why ain't you mad at the Klu Klux Klan instead of the people your Uncle Bill was trying to help get free?"

A cloud come over him right then, or maybe a demon crawled up his back, like they usta say in church is all around and making people do bad things like smoke and drink and lay with harlots and wear makeup if you're a girl. He had me one side of the kitchen to the other and back again with my feet way off the ground, hollering how there ain't no son of his standing up for spicks and niggas and jews. They all stepped in with a beer to make him calm down and let me go, and pretty soon he's sitting at the dining room table, singing that funny song about "cigareets and rye whiskey and wild, wild women."

Knowing he won't remember none of what I said or what

he did when he gets off the drunk, I disappear right there in the house for a few days until he gets back to work. That's what I mean when I say I already know how to be invisible. It's like you can be reading a comic book, and if you keep an ear out when he's walking or stomping around the house, you just go quiet into the room he ain't in. Acourse, if that don't work, you skedaddle, and then it's up to the woods, which is a lot more fun than comics anyways.

So after I figure this all out, I just walk down the hall, pretending I ain't afraid of them bullies. Like, I walk right by them, and if they trip me up or punch my back or pinch my arm, I just say quiet, "Oh hi, Jeb," or "Hey there, Stu." The real trick is pretending you ain't hurt when they get you good. And you gotta keep it up until it all dies down and goes away. Which pretty soon it does, because bullies don't get no kick outta hurting you when you don't put on a show and make everybody look at them and think how big and tough they are. They figure like, what's the point of pounding on a nobody that gets nobody looking at you?

Sure enough, it ain't too long before my way of thinking pays off. I'm going down the hall walking by a bunch of bullies, and one of them points at me and says, "Hey, here comes The Kid Who Doesn't Care." I walk right on by them, looking down. "Hey Joe. Hey Stu. Hey Bill." They all laugh, but none of them pinches or punches or trips me up. When I get down the hall, I hear one of them say, "Ya know, in a funny sorta way, them Gordon kids are kinda tough."

It's true there's a kinda tough you get when people pound or pick on you a lot. It's not the outside kinda tough, though. It's the inside kinda tough that lets you look blank at them so they can't tell what you're really feeling because what you're feeling is pushed way down. Acourse, you don't ever say what you're really feeling or what you really want to do to them or they'll go after you. Mosta the time, you don't even say it to yourself.

The way I see it is we all got different ways of getting through. Junior's got his thing with all them girls, and Johnny goes in for the first punch. Me, I'm just a nobody, walking the halls, looking down, and nothing you ever do's gonna matter because I'm the kid who doesn't care. And that's the way it goes for me. At least until I'm big enough to say different.

CHAPTER 30

SOMEWHERES IN tHE MIDDLE

Dear Missus Hollister,

I wanted to tell you that Junior died, but we ain't supposed to talk about it or Ma will feel bad. I bet by now you're dead too, so you won't be telling nobody what I say. I hope you didn't get so old you got sick like Missus Farnsworth and you had trouble just dragging around like she did. If she was still alive and you ain't dead, you could talk to her and hear about them three wars she was in and how she wasn't afraid of getting killed, and when they was dropping bombs and shooting at her, she helped the soldiers anyway. I know you didn't fight in wars or you would've told us in class. But you were a good teacher to me, and you thought I was the best boy ever, even though I ain't.

I wrote the stories like you said, and Daddy found them behind the wall when he was fixing it so the snow stops blowing through the house. He said, "What's this, your homework?" and he flipped through the pages, but he didn't read it because his glasses wasn't on and I never saw him read anyway, but Ma says he can. And he does math in his head faster than Jean and she's valatorian.

I can't write no more Missus Hollister, because all I can do is think of Junior and how he went away and never came back. But Jean came back from teaching because she was sad

191

about Junior's accident and missing us. It just don't seem real, like nothing ever does. I got happy the other day because Jean was home, and I forgot that he was dead, and I came running down the stairs and I called out loud for him to come and teach me baseball.

When it hit me he was dead, I stopped halfway down the stairs and got stuck in that place for a long, long time. When they hear me call his name, they all stop talking down there, and nobody comes to help because Charlotte said later it was like I slapped them all, and they was taking care of Ma.

I knew right then that I could be as mean as Daddy ever was, even if I didn't mean to. And I thought how maybe Junior didn't mean it when he picked on us, or Daddy doesn't mean it when he scares us so, or Mommy when she don't come home. There's things inside that make people do what they do, and if they could see them things maybe they wouldn't do them, and nobody would ever feel bad or hurt no one or get hurt and die like Junior.

When I was stuck on the stairs, I thought that I was dying, too. I fell back into this cave-like thing where I was all alone and could only feel that bad about what I did. And the angels was down there growling, but it was really coming outta me. And I say to myself that I ain't ever gonna come out and make them look at me again, because I forgot that Junior died and made them all remember.

But then it was like Junior comes over to me and says, "Alright Fuzzy Head, you can stay down here with me but you got to go back there too and make like it's okay. And when you grow up, you'll look like me and talk like me and comb your hair like me and that will make them happy." So I snapped out of it right then and jumped the stairs like Mary and ran out the door fast so I couldn't see them cry.

I go running across the road where Junior used to climb and I jump the ditch like I never could before and dig my fingers into his big old tree and claw and climb up to the first branch. And up I go, way up, where he says you can see the world—and today maybe you can, because most of the leaves is down.

I look down and see that Bev and Charlotte is coming after me, but I don't answer when they call. They stop when they get to the ditch and look around, but they don't look up because they know I don't ever climb. I see they both was feeling bad. Charlotte knows that I'm somewheres near and so she starts to talk to me. "Frankie!" She says, "Frankie! Come on home now. We've got something to tell you."

I know they're gonna tell me how I hurt Ma and yell at me not to do it again, so I just hide up there in the branches. When I close my eyes, I can see Ma in the house laying down with a washcloth on her face and the big and little kids all around, holding her and everyone telling everyone how bad I was.

Just then Bev hollers out, "Frankie! It's President Kennedy! He's dead! Someone shot him!"

Them words make me dizzy, and when I look down it scares me I climbed so high. So I just hug into the tree, and when I do, it starts swaying back and forth and back and forth like it was the hand of God trying to throw me off. And maybe it was, Missus Hollister, because of all the bad things I said at God when they told me Junior died. But I dig my fingers in real tight and hold on until he gets tired and goes away. And when the tree stops swaying, I laugh and say, "There you go, Fuzzy Head—you beat him out!"

It takes me a long time to scootch down that tree, but when I'm coming down and the bottom gets closer, I can feel me getting strong. I know right then that I don't need nobody to help me no more, because I'm big, and they could all go away and never come back and I would still be strong.

When I go inside, I see Daddy sitting in the corner and how he's scrunched over and how he don't look so big and how he don't look at me because of the things he said to Junior before he raced off in the car and got himself killed when it tipped over and rolled on top of him. They kept him alive for two weeks and wouldn't let me in to see him because he looked so bad, and Johnny said there was all this beeping noise and wires was everywhere and some of them was going in and out of him. So I stayed home like they told me and went up to the woods to be alone and call the fire down on Junior so he'd jump up and come back home and maybe play with us or even pick on us, I don't care.

But the fire don't come down no matter what I say or pray or yell at God or promise how good I'll be if he makes Junior get up like Jesus did that time in the Bible when his friend was in that cave four days all dead and he was stinking. Then one day Jean calls us kids together and tells us Junior died, which set off all this crying and wailing like you don't ever want to hear.

Later, when Jean ain't looking, I snitch a pack of Ma and Daddy's camel cigarettes and run off to the woods and smoke them down until it makes me sick and dizzy and then I smoke some more until I have to puke it out. I was laying on my side almost asleep when a squirrel pops up and looks at me off to the side like they do and sets me off to laughing, which I guess was really just a different way of crying.

So now I'm mad at Daddy, and when I look at him sitting in that corner I hate him real bad. But maybe there's a sorry for him in there too because I know when he hollered at Junior so many times he was only trying to make him be good and not drive fast and drink like a maniac when he went out. But Daddy don't know how to do it soft like Ma does because when he grew up men were men like he always says and they don't act like boys or sissies. So he just blows up like he always does when something ticks him off and he says some awful bad things to Junior. Ma says it was Daddy killed him, not the car.

Now it's like Ma don't want to live no more, so we got to take care of her because Daddy don't know how to do that neither. And the whole world is sad and crying too, even the rich ones like Missus Kennedy with that black thing across her face and little John-boy when the horses pull his daddy right on by. I hope he's too little to know it's his daddy in that box with the flag on and he ain't ever coming back, like Junior.

When they make me go to school again, I dream I hopped a train to California and I was riding on top, and my hair was happy-like, and when the teacher's talking I'm riding through the states with the sun and clouds and trees and all the pretty horses running by. It's good to get away for just that much, so I take the dreaming to my other classes, and instead of making the monsters small like Charlotte says to do, I make the pretty big—and when the teachers see me smiling, they think that I'm gonna be alright from Junior dying—or maybe they think I'm just a little crazy, but I don't care.

When I dream like that, it's kinda like that tree up on the mountain. You know it's beautiful, but you can't always go there, and it ain't always there anyway, because sometimes it's winter or fall when all the leaves is gone. But you can make it inside whenever you want, and even if it's sissy, nobody knows because it's deep inside where nobody else can go. You just breathe it into you and it comes right back to life, and you can even make the birds come back and fly around and kiss.

And that's kinda like what I do when I write, Missus Hollister. I make it real inside before it comes out and I write it down in stories. So I guess I will keep right on writing after all, because that's a thing I like to do. At first it was you that made me do it. But now it's Junior and Johnny and Pearl and Gracey and Mary and all the rest of us that's stuck here between good and bad—even Ma and Daddy. And I was thinking how maybe I'm not the only one that's somewheres in the middle. Maybe it's the bunch of us.

CHAPTER 31

HoW I Got tHRouGH It

Junior's been gone a long, long time now—like almost two years—and so I think I'll write about how he got me through it—not Junior, but the dog, I mean—Chow. It just don't seem real how he came to me and when he did and what we did together every day that summer and for the next long time, and how he got me outta the house and away from the dark and pain of Junior's dying and into something way more like what boys are supposed to do.

I had taken to clearing outta the house anyways when things got bad—I mean with Daddy. Or when Ma looked at me the way she did, off I'd go across the road to where Junior used to climb. Well, this one day I come across his favorite tree which I know I can climb now, just like he used to—with a jump and a pull and yanking up of my body. But just when I walk up to the tree, this old memory comes back and makes me look down on the ground instead of up. And so I walk around the tree trunk, kicking up the leaves and dirt.

And there it is—Charlotte's old flat stone that I had put there right after Junior buried our baby brother by this here very tree. It's worked its way into the ground a bit, so I wiggle it out and take a look at it, and when I do the whole day of when the baby died comes right to life on that stone, and all the sadness of it, too. Since I got no water to clean it off, I tug my shirt over my head and use it to rub the stone all clean and dry. The shovel Junior left there way back then is fallen to the ground and lays off to the side, all rusted over.

I'm brushing old dead leaves away, looking for a little piece of rock sharp enough to write the baby's name with, and I get to thinking about how some people don't really want to live and other people really want to die, and if there's a difference. I figure on this side of things maybe there is a difference and it matters, but on that side maybe not, because no matter how you get yourself buried, you're just as dead, whether you was thinking about not wanting to live or wanting to die. Before you did die, I mean. So you're dead anyways, except to the people who keep seeing you after you die and then remember what you was like. So maybe it only matters to them what you was thinking before you did die, and whether you just didn't want to live or whether you really did want to die. But I ain't thinking clear about any of that.

I can't find a sharp enough rock, so I take my jackknife out and begin to scratch and dig the baby's name into the stone. I say to myself this time it'll stay on there for good. It was a hot, hot day and that little bit of work with no water made me sweat and get a little dizzy. I hear squirrels scampering through the woods, and it makes me wonder where they get their water.

Junior's been gone too long for me to be seeing him so much, but the tree rustles above and he's in it, way up there swaying back and forth, one leg and one arm hooked into the tree, the others waving in the wind. The bending of his body out and in, in and out, keeps the tree swaying near the top. The smell of earth and old dead leaves is in the forest everywhere.

How is it you can see someone who's not even here anymore better than when he was here? It's because in a way he still is here, I guess. Ma can't turn around but what she sees him standing there with his crooked smile and nice combed hair. And she sees him inside of Johnny and me, which makes her look away, and then I know it's time to get gone so's not to make her any sadder. Maybe that's why Johnny quit school and joined the Marines in Vietnam, so she won't have to look at him. I know that's why I spend so much time in these here woods.

As I scratch away with my little knife, there's a fever in me I can't get out—but I can feel it when I cut into the stone and see the baby's name. I remember thinking if I slipped and cut myself it might be halfway good, and maybe it would even feel good, like when Ma threw herself out the car. Bev says it was on a slow turn, so it's not like she really wants to die. It's more like she just don't really want to live. And the kind of pain you feel when you hit the ground makes you not even feel the worser pain inside. The girls and Gramma took care of Ma all day and made Daddy stay downstairs. He swears they wasn't fighting when she tumbled out.

Their staying away got longer, not shorter, after Junior died—just the opposite of what I thought would happen— but that don't matter. We fend for ourselves pretty good when they're away. It's just that missing them feels real heavy when they're gone. But then we feel it even more when they come home and they ain't really home. It's like something keeps pulling them or pushing them away from the house. Maybe it's Junior himself, I don't know. Or maybe it's them wondering why he up and died. I just know there's something in the air that pulls all of us away from the house and away from each other. It ain't enough—like it used to be—that we're all alive together. Well, we ain't, with Junior gone.

So it's not the baby's name so much as all this sickness I'm gashing into the stone when it happens quick—the shaking of a nearby bush. And then this deep and long and gravelly growl. The bush shakes again—this time closer—and I feel the fear of God they talk about. And just like that, he's right there in the clearing—like a beam of light—the biggest and most beautiful dog I've ever seen. And the scariest, too.

There's a half-dead woodchuck hanging from his mouth— he must have carried it from the field. Poor thing's gasping for air and kicking out a few last breaths. The dog don't pay the woodchuck no nevermind for glaring at me. He growls and steps toward me, then stops. He leaps into the air and gives the woodchuck a final ripping and throwing about, then drops him off to one side dead as a rock—a cold-blooded killing right before my eyes.

I stand up slow. He stares at me. I freeze in place. Then he wags his bushy tail, which is the kind that curls up and touches his back. I know the next move is mine. I start to breathe again, and my first steps toward him are forced—short and choppy. I kneel slow in front of him and begin to stroke his face, steady but firm, how any dog would like. I run my fingers down his neck and across his back as far as I can reach, then wrap my arms around his neck and start to sniffle, then to cry. His hair's so thick you can't even feel his bones. His legs hold up the weight of me. Right then I tell him how it's gonna be with me and him from then on. "You're my dog." I tell him over and over. "You're mine."

He stands there in place on his rock-solid legs until he gets tired of me sniveling, then licks the wet from my face. It makes me laugh for the first time since Junior died. He knows we have the rest of our lives to know each other but only so much time to hunt, so he pushes on. I grab my jackknife and shirt and off we go, doing for the rest of that day and into the night what we would do for the next long time—running and hunting and searching through all the hills around the house, looking for some wild animal to sniff out and track and chase and, if we got lucky, kill.

Woodchucks—especially woodchucks—rabbits, squirrels, and even some birds, like grouse and pheasants—we chase and hunt them all and kill what we can. Acourse, it wasn't me that did the killing, but I got pretty good at chasing things out for him to run down and mangle. And it's me that climbs the trees to chase down a squirrel that scrambles up there when he comes on the run. Or I stomp on a pile of brush or tip it over to scare a rabbit out. Or I grab a stick and help him dig a woodchuck out that he chases down a hole. Or I start a fire over the hole to smoke him out.

After a while I know when he's hungry, and I make a slit and spill the guts and cut and pull the skin off some dead thing he's killed and I figure he'll eat. I pull the meat off the bones and feed it to him in little pieces, all raw and bloody. If I get hungry myself, I build a little fire and cook and eat what he ain't mangled too much—mostly rabbits and squirrels, but sometimes a wild bird. I light up a smoke I snitched from the house while the meat cooks, or sometimes I take a nap, using his belly as a pillow. He knows all the streams and takes me to them for a drink when the time is right. We lay on our bellies and lap it up together.

I named him Chow that first day when I brung him home and Daddy checked him over. He says it's a purebred because the inside of his mouth is all black and his tongue is turning dark purple. He says he's from Alaska because his fur's so thick and they got a breed there that's called a Chow with a sort of pushed-in nose like this one here. And the color's right—a golden light brown with black outlines like the devil. Daddy stands back and looks at him and says how that may be the best dam good-looking dog he's ever seen. I say how his name is Chow so Daddy can think he named him. He says you can call him what you want, but he ain't staying.

So I say he stays or I'll run off with him because I know Daddy can't take another loss. Daddy looks at me hard, and then rubs my head and says okay you can keep him, but don't you dare bring him in the house or feed him because he'll eat us outta house and home. So I say we get our own food in the woods, and he says that's why he's got blood all through his teeth and smells like death. He says to keep him away from the little kids because a Chow's a jealous dog around food, and they do best with just one owner. Later at school, I look up Chow in their books about dogs, and everything Daddy said about him is true.

For the next long time, there was Chow and only Chow. He's mine and I'm his, and God help any other dog that tries to get near me. He rips into them like wrapping paper on Christmas. And none of the other kids dare get near him either because I was just as jealous of him as he was of me. One time, Pearl says I don't play with the little kids no more, and I tell her there's too much hunting we got to do. She laughs and says it's funny when I talk crazy.

We live to run the fields and hills, and when I get better at kicking out the game, he lets me take the lead. I tell him to stay while I make a big circle, swinging my club until a rabbit or whatever jumps up. I yell out, "Kill!" and he's on it! Ain't no dog ever could tear up the ground like Chow. It's the meanest charge, it's bite and rip and slash and throw down and pick back up and throw again and then it's over. The growls that come outta him is downright scary and make me so proud that he's mine.

It was Chow that made me hate school so much. The only reason I didn't quit was Jean came back to teach, and I didn't want to make her look bad like Johnny did. So I'd sit there in back of the class every day drawing pictures of Chow and me fighting off monsters and killing stuff. I couldn't think about no schoolwork because I was afraid of him getting bored at home and taking off because I was away from him too much. Or maybe some guy who thinks he owns him would come by and grab him back. Or maybe some hunter would shoot him for chasing deer, and when I come home he's all bloody and dying.

So every day I begged Ma to watch him while I was off to school. She said she would, which gave her something to do and not feel so sad. And then at night I'd make her tell me what he did all day when I was gone. One time she tells me Chow was sitting down in the field a long time and wouldn't come up when she called. So she went down to where he was, and he was sitting with a bunch of baby rabbits between his paws, licking on them like he was their mommy. She says she never seen nothing like it. I figured maybe he killed their mommy, but I didn't say that to Ma because she sees Chow all kind and gentle, which he was to her.

One time, the teacher makes us write this made-up story they call fiction, but I wrote mine true about Chow and how big he is, and how beautiful, and how I like to run behind him when we go on hunts, and how we kill, and how we eat what we kill when we get hungry. I figured they're all sissies so they won't know what I wrote was true, but when I'm done, one of them smart alecks says "So that's why you come to school with all them scratches!" And another dum-dum points at my shirt and says, "That there's blood!"

So the teacher calls me up to her desk later and says how she's bothered by what I wrote and asks me am I sure it's fiction and if I'm really eating animals in the woods. I got eight sisters so I know how to listen when ladies talk, and I can see by how she says it that Chow and me was headed for trouble. So I laugh and ask her how can a boy and a dog catch rabbits without a gun? She takes my arms and looks at all the scratches on them, then looks at the blood on my shirt, which I tell her is ketchup from lunch. She puts the back of her hand on my forehead and says it seems like I been losing weight.

And so that's the last time I let anyone know about Chow and how we tear the mountains up. But after that it got worse for Chow and me. Daddy says no more ramming over the hills for me, and when I jump off the bus, it's straight to the house and eat. He says I'll be getting worms from eating wild animals, and if I catch you smoking I'll wring your little neck. He didn't lick me like he never does. He says he'll get me a gun so I can go hunting right—but I don't want nothing that will slow us down, so I never press him for it.

I knew Chow would take off and leave me if we didn't hunt, so I took to hunting at night, which was easy when Ma and

Daddy wasn't home but took more sneaking when they was. Acourse, the animals good for killing ain't out at night, just the ones you don't want around, like skunks and porcupines and raccoons, and they all get the rabies from bats which is flying everywhere.

If you ever seen that movie Old Yeller, you know what happens to dogs that get the rabies and how it makes everyone cry when they put him down. So we do go hunting at night, but I make sure to keep him moving through the woods and across the fields. He don't get it why we're running all over them hills like that and not stopping to kill, but by now he loves me like I do him and he follows me anywheres.

One night we're way up there on a hill when Chow takes off after a deer, and that's the last I ever see of him. I like to think he went off and found another kid to hunt with, but it seems more likely some guy up there jacklighting deer shot at him for chasing off his game, and off Chow runs, never to come home again. I call for him, but he's way gone, and I'm up there alone in the middle of all these trees, and the moon ain't out so you can't even see.

If you've ever been in the woods at night, you know they come alive if you stand in one place. And now I'm afraid to call out for him or some big animal will jump out after me. Right then, shaking under all them trees, I see how I ain't brave without Chow, and how I was using him to make me feel tough, and only if he comes back will I be brave again. Under all them big trees with wild animals crawling all around, I see how I ain't never gonna be brave like Daddy, knocking people down in bar fights, or like Junior with all them girls and driving fast, or even like Johnny going to fight in Vietnam. Right then it seems like maybe I'm supposed to die in these here woods, like by getting rabies or tripping into some deep hole or falling down from some high tree. I look around for Junior to show up like he used to before Chow came along, but all I see is the eyes of those animals shining and blinking and staring at me in the woods all dark.

Pretty soon I figure out that if I move my feet a little and then make my legs take baby steps, and if I pick up a stick and swing it, I can get brave enough to walk back down to the house. So that's what I do, but I'm crying all the way—and not just because I'm scared, but because I know Chow is gone and ain't ever coming back.

There's fog laying over the house like a tired ghost when I come down over the mountain. The black of the house is poking through it, and I can see early morning lights in what windows is showing.

They can't make me go to school for the next few days, and I don't talk, so Ma and Daddy go in to meet with the teachers about what's going on with me. Daddy comes home real mad at all them teachers and Mister Klump. He hollers at Ma, "What do they know! Detached! What the hell is that! That kid can do a whole pile a mixed fractions in his head!" Ma says, "Attached. They said he don't make attachments."

Ma comes in to where I was laying and rubs my head. She says how there's always people in this world that want to ruin it for little kids, and how it's up to me think how I want to think and not to let them spoil it. She says they only know what they think they know, and just remember they can't see inside you even though they might think they can. She says it was me and her took care of Chow together, and she'll never forget how he took care of them baby rabbits or that time he chased all them robbers down the hill.

So the next day they made me go to school and then they made me stay after so the bunch of them could talk to me. All the teachers was there, and Mister Klump, and some lady who makes little kids feel better by talking to them. She says how they been looking into things and come to see how I might just need a little help getting plugged in and making friends, and how it might be time to turn off what's been going on inside my head which is keeping me from joining in. She says giving up things is part of growing up, like the Easter Bunny or Santa or even pretend dogs.

She pulls out the pile of pictures I drawed of Chow fighting monsters and killing stuff in the woods and says how these was all stuffed in my different desks, but there wasn't no sign of homework. Then she asks me all these questions about what's real and what's not real to see if I could tell the difference. Right then I remember what Ma said about how they only know what they think they know, and I figured just because they can't see what I can see don't mean what I can see ain't real. But I don't say none of that to them because they only want me to do more homework—which I should do anyways so Jean don't look stupid for having me as a brother.

I knew none of them ever had a dog or loved a dog or lost a dog like Chow. So I knew not to say how it makes you sick to think of how beautiful he is running through the woods with his hair like gold on fire, and how he charges into all them animals snapping with that scary growl, and how every kill is just so perfect, and how it made me special to be picked by him and to own him all myself. So I just let them talk on and on like big people always do anyways.

The lady who makes kids feel better was telling me how good my drawing was and how she's gonna sign me up for art that's healthy and after-school clubs like chess so's I can play with real-life kids. Mister Klump sits there jingling his keys like he's ready to go, so pretty soon they cut it off, but not before all the teachers got a chance to say how good I was or how bad I was in different classes. I figure I can do the same to them, but I keep it shut.

When I come out the door, there's Jean waiting to drive me home. She says when she was little, she had a friend in her head that would take her all around the world on vacations so's she could get a break from taking care of everything and everybody. She says in a funny way it helped her become valatorian, because when she come back from vacation she'd work twice as hard on homework. I tell her I bet that's why Daddy says you're crazy smart, and she laughs her head off at that.

So that's all there is to say about how I got through it—Junior dying I mean. When Chow left, I could see him really clear for a long time, but then he sorta faded off like fog does when you walk in it, and it's harder and harder to bring him back. And pretty soon I see I can't make Junior come back when I want, because he's got a life of his own, and he shows up when he knows the time is right for him and me both, just like he did when he was alive. Most the time he was off doing his own thing like chasing girls and driving fast and smoking and drinking and having fun, but he came back when I needed him, and I guess it's the same way now he's dead.

The other day we was playing chess after school, and the kids was mad at me for beating them so bad and being new.

The teacher Mister Jamison looks at me in front of them all and says this is about teamwork, not smashing down your friends. So I figure I'll have to dummy it down to make them feel good. When they was yapping at me like they was, I says to myself at them, "You're the ones detached, not me, getting so mad about a stupid game, like it's real life."

But then I felt sorta sorry for them too, because I can tell by the way they dress up that they ain't ever really lived, like me with twelve kids in the family and learning how to make it on your own. And they ain't never run through the woods and over the fields with a dog so beautiful as Chow, and so lit up for life as he was, even in all that killing. Right then it's clear to me maybe that's how real life is supposed to be lived if you dare to live it and don't haul off and throw yourself away.

"Mister Jamison," I say loud enough so they all can hear. "I ain't really all that good at chess, I just been real lucky."

He smiles and winks at me and says, "Welcome to the group, Mister Gordon. I think you'll do just fine."

I smile back at him like I know he wants me to, but I look around at all them nerds with shiny shoes and think about what he just said, and the whole thing sorta gives me the creeps, ya know?

EPILOGUE

Just finished reading all my old stories that Yvonne sent off to me. God, what a little nerd I was! I mean what kid would spend his playtime writing stories just to prove he's the best boy ever to a teacher who's probably dead anyway? If I ever get out of this hole they call Nam, maybe I'll turn them stories into a little book, I don't know. Hell, maybe I'll read a few of the chapters to the guys some night. But then again, maybe I won't. It's like they're way too personal. About the family, I mean. And when I wrote them, I didn't know which way was up. I mean, what kid does? One day I'll write a book called, "The Way It Really Was." Now that would be a laugh.

Sometimes at night when the casualties are coming slow, we sit around and read our local papers to each other. We focus on the 'socialite' sections, and it really tears us up. I mean what passes for social life in the small towns most of these soldiers come from is a regular riot. "Sister so-and-so visited aunt whoever last Sunday after church" —that sort of thing. Brought a baked casserole. When the southern boys play up their southern twangs, it really cracks you up. Throw in a few beers and you're rolling on the floor.

I'm just so sick of all the blood and guts. Just give me a section 8 and be done with it. But they've got ways of keeping you around—shuffle you here and there, put you in a softer killing zone—that sort of thing. Could put in for a transfer, but in the end you're still in this rat hole. So why trade all the buddies you've collected for a transfer, when the blood and dying is everywhere. Seems like that's what we're really all about—blood and dying.

I hope Johnny holds tight until I get home. We'll talk it out then. God, just don't let him re-enlist! Getting drafted is one thing—I can live with that. (Hell, I am living with that!) But joining up for another tour is just bananas. Thank God I'm not getting shot at every day like he did, and I haven't been wounded like he was. But I do have an idea of what he went through then by what I see happening to these boys now. Beg him if you have to, just keep him home.

The pull-out is happening just like Tricky Dick said it would—this "just and lasting peace." Except there's more of us getting killed now than before that grand announcement. Unless they shoot down the silver bird they put me on to fly me out of here, I will come home. And I will be there for Johnny. And Don and Robbie and all the rest of us suckers that was conned or coerced into this hellhole.

There was this boy the other day. Two nights ago I think it was. I don't know, I haven't slept. The choppers just keep on bringing them in, and they say to get your asses off to the ER. But they don't have to tell us. The sound of those blades chopping through the air cuts right through you too, and you can almost see the bodies piled up before they land. Sometimes you just wish they'd come under fire and divert to someplace else. Sergeant Darcy says it's all good time, meaning no matter what you do over here, it's just one day closer to getting home, so don't let none of it get to you.

But it's not good time. Not when you see what's happening to these poor boys. Gerry broke down the other day and tells Sergeant Darcy not to tell him their names. He doesn't want to know their names. The sergeant gave him the night off and says to the rest of us we'll have to pick up the slack. And we was okay with that. But at the time I was puzzled by what Gerry said.

There was this boy two nights ago and his lights was going out. We all knew we'd never get him to surgery fast enough. So we stand around the gurney holding onto him, saying what we can. But he's away off somewhere. The nurses are holding back tears, and I find myself breathing really slow and deep and hard so I won't break down in front of them. I can tell by looking at his chin, he doesn't shave. I mean he doesn't have to shave. And he has pimples on his forehead like you get in seventh grade.

He starts calling for his mama like they do. This long, slow wail that comes from a place he didn't even know was in him. There's a drawl in it, I think—not too deeply southern, though. Kentucky, North Carolina. We let go of him and grab onto each other like there's some power in the bunch of us to keep him on this side of things. There's a longing in his cry that takes me into falling back like I do. Back to home and the everlasting pull of it. And the only thing I see clear to do is to take his body to the creek.

The little kids are screaming upstream and the big kids are playing way down. So I float him off to one side where the water's not too deep and runs so slow. And Junior comes over and helps me hold him back into the water so it washes all the smell and mud and muck and bullet holes away. Something in me says to push him off and let the water take him under and away, but Junior says there's a few that we'll hang on to, and this here boy is one. He looks at me and smiles, cups the back of my head. "You ain't Fuzzy Head no more."

When I come back into it, it's me that's cleaning up the body, or the best that I can do with what I've got. I see his dog tags on the tray and resist the urge to scarf them up. There's a responsibility in taking on a name like that, and it never really washes off. So Gerry's right. And Junior's right. I'll keep him with me long enough. But I won't take on his name, won't own him in that way. When they took him all covered up away, he was just a body like the rest of them. I listened to the gurney creaking down the hall and thought how it ain't the dead ones that get to you, it's the dying.

When they finally let me off, it's still dark outside but heading toward the morning light. There's dankness in the air, probably what always happens after monsoon. The floodlights over the compound create a cozy umbrella of warmth and security that belies what's really happening here. I allow myself to take some comfort in it. That part of me will never die, I guess, the part that escapes into illusion.

I got a care package from home the other day, and jumbled in with all the other stuff was this picture of the house with Johnny and Daddy on a scaffold, putting siding on. They was coming down from the peak with this pretty blue board and waving at me for the camera. Below the scaffolding, lots of happy grandkids was running all around. Ma was standing in the picture window, arms crossed, cigarette in hand, staring far away at who knows what. Some car on the highway I suppose. In the parts of the house beneath the scaffold, the old black of the house was showing through, the black I had come to dread, especially in my teenage years, when I waited for the bus full of kids and all those prying eyes.

As I held the picture in my hands, it began to shake with a life of its own. It tore from my grip and fell to the floor. Some power in the world around me forced a steady calm, walked me slowly out the door, and leaned me into to a pile of sandbags all worn out and crumbling. Just then I heard the far-off voice of little Frankie saying how you'll go crazy if you think two ways about the same thing. Especially going home.

Before I could even mull on it, Sergeant Darcy walked on past me. He stopped, turned around, and snapped his fingers at me. "Good God, Gordon! You look like shit! Just do your job and get the hell out of here. And stop your gull-dam thinking!"

I looked at him, smiled, then broke into a laugh. "Best advice I've heard all day." He walks over to me and slaps my shoulder. He lights a cigarette and inhales deeply. His exhale reeks of self-satisfaction. "God, don't you just love this place." Then he pokes me. "Hey, Gordon! Rustle up a bunch of guys to replace these sandbags. You know where the new ones are."

Hard and easy. Heavy and light. Rocks and feathers. That's just life. Maybe that's living. The pain and love of it. And if you don't have both, you're dead, or wished you were. Or maybe it's better to be halfway in the dark, like little Frankie. Where the lies bring you comfort and not knowing which way is up is a sort of kindness.

That night in the barracks this thing came up in me, like a poem, though I ain't ever wrote one, except those ones we did in Missus Roger's classes, most of which I skipped.

WONDERING CHILD

Author Unknown

Wondering Child
Watch with me
Snow falls by the darkened glass
And nearing lights portray
The joyous white descent

Bless you
Little fuzzy head
Nose atop the sill
Wide and sleepy eyes
Lost in framed remembrance

Watch with me
Warm cheek pressed
Against the frosted pane
There is mercy
In covered tracks
And the windswept blur
Of haloes

Fear not
The murmuring of angels
Who shall appear unwinged
Servants at your door

I signed the thing, "Author Unknown," because the words were not really mine. I must have read them or heard them somewhere else, I don't really know. I mean they ain't the sort of words I would ever pull together myself. Unless there's someone living in me that's got a life of his own. Like little Frankie. But he's too young to write a poem like that. Maybe it's the voice of Junior wanting to come back. Or the dying soldier boys who live in me like ghosts. Anyway, the writing of it gives me a quiet sort of satisfaction, even though it don't dish out any answers. Hell, nobody I know's got any answers. At least none that I'd be quick to believe.

About the Author

Frank Gordon (pen name) was born in Susquehanna, Pennsylvania and raised on a hill in upstate New York. After graduating from high school, he was drafted into the US Army where he served as a medic in Vietnam. Using the GI Bill, he obtained a BA in Creative Writing and thereafter worked in the field of human services until retirement. A widower, he now spends time visiting his three grown children, oil painting, and writing. *Somewheres in the Middle* is his first published book. A sequel, tentatively titled, *The Way It Really Was*, is planned for publication in 2020.

Made in the USA
Middletown, DE
11 April 2020